796.35762   Burroughs, Jeff.
Burroughs   The little team
            that could.

DATE DUE			

THE LITTLE TEAM THAT COULD

Jeff Burroughs
with
Tom Hennessy

Bonus Books, Inc., Chicago

98 97 96 95 94   5 4 3 2 1

Library of Congress Catalog Card Number: 94-70385

International Standard Book Number: 1-56625-008-0

Bonus Books, Inc.
160 East Illinois Street
Chicago, Illinois 60611

*Front cover photo of Charlie Hayes and back cover photo of the Long Beach
All-Stars courtesy of Hillary Sloss/Press-Telegram*

Typesetting by Point West, Inc., Carol Stream, IL

Printed in the United States of America

*Dedicated to the memory of
Ruben Gutierrez*

Contents

Part One

However badly kids behave, there is one piece of knowledge, one certainty, that enables the adults around them to
survive.

They know that sooner or later (almost always
later) even the most delinquent of little guys will fall
asleep.

It was long past midnight by the time the 13 little
delinquents on our bus finally drifted away to dreamland.
The relief was tremendous. I felt the way America feels
when the State of the Union address ends or when sports-
caster Dick Vitale signs off.

As the bus rolled through the darkness of central
Pennsylvania, I sat back and relished the silence. I had al-

most forgotten how terrific silence can be. For 15 hours since we left Southern California, I had listened to shouts, screams, sobs, shrieks, screeches, badly imitated barnyard sounds, and, now and then, the poignant whoosh of a nervôus kid throwing up.

I had heard flight attendants sigh and rugged-looking pilots drop their square jaws to ask, "Who the hell are these kids?" Inside terminals, I had heard passengers cry out in pain as the boys stepped on outstretched ankles while in the throes of a spirited game of Terminal Tag.

The worst part of this trouble-fraught odyssey was a layover to change planes in St. Louis. Denny Mayfield, one of the three adults chaperoning the kids, tried valiantly to entertain them with card tricks. The kids were entranced. For about 20 seconds.

Next thing we knew, they were doing 100-yard dashes in an area where passengers were boarding a plane. Or attempting to board a plane.

Then they pitched coins against walls, gambling for money in public like delinquent Dead End Kids. It was West Side Story without music and switchblades. This was followed by their terrorist phase, in which they tried to commandeer those electric vehicles used to transport passengers inside terminals.

Through most of this, I stared at a paperback. By pretending to read, I figured others in the terminal would think I had no connection to the tiny savages who now seemed on the verge of dismantling the St. Louis airport.

But in truth, I was very connected to those savages, almost as if they were my own kids, which, in fact, one of them was. The St. Louis 13 (as I began to picture them advertised on "Wanted" posters in post offices) were, in reality, a baseball team called the Long Beach (California) All-Stars. Two days earlier, they had become the Little League champions of the entire western United States.

So what if they were as loud, boisterous and mischievous as kids can get? Over the past couple of months, I had come to know and love every one of them. And when they were not cartwheeling through airports and otherwise driving adults crazy—man, could they play baseball!

I should know. I was their coach.

As some of you might guess, coaching Little League is a thing you do when life gets dull and you decide to spice it up by risking your job, marriage, car, lower back, community standing, credit rating, financial security, and sanity. On the Occupational Insanity Scale, Little League coach ranks somewhere between alligator wrestler and the guy in the Dracula films who sits in a cell and munches bugs.

My own involvement in Little League was an inevitable consequence of my love for baseball. Briefly put, my background is this: I was born Jeffrey Alan Burroughs on March 7, 1951, in Long Beach. As far back as I can remember, I played baseball.

For 16 seasons, I played it in the major leagues—for six teams (Washington, Texas, Atlanta, Seattle, Oakland and Toronto) and for 13 managers, if you count Ted Turner, who, in 1977, managed the Braves for one game (and to our amazement, won it).

In 1974, I played well enough with the Texas Rangers to be named the Most Valuable Player in the American League. In 1985, my last season, I was a member of the Toronto Blue Jays that won the American League's eastern division championship.

Yet all of that was a mere warm-up for my second and crazier baseball career, the one in Little League. Nothing in my 1,689 major-league games prepared me for the greater challenges of the smaller league, such as escorting those 13 little rascals across the continental United States.

It was August 22, 1992. We were on our way to the World Series.

Let me be sure you understand which World Series is involved here. I am not talking about that seven-game, heavy-duty, major-league, billion-dollar extravaganza they sometimes call the "October Classic." I am talking about the other World Series, the one fans frequently stumble across while flipping the channels in search of something—anything—having to do with sports.

I am talking about the Little League World Series in Williamsport, Pennsylvania.

You may recognize it also as the World Series that for years—no, decades—was dominated by kids from Asia. Back then, no one talked a great deal about why those kids seemed to play baseball so much better than our kids. Oh, there were a few theories about Asian players. They were more motivated, they played the game year-round, they were more disciplined, etcetera after nauseating etcetera.

But no one talked much about the oddest aspect of this phenomenon. After proving their baseball mastery in Williamsport, where kids compete at ages 11 through 13, the boys from Asia went home and slipped into obscurity. They were never heard from again. At least, not by us.

Take, for example, Taiwan, the most dominant country in Little League World Series competition. With less than one-tenth of the population of the United States, Taiwan nevertheless won the world championship 15 times between 1969 and 1981. And five times between 1986 and 1991.

Were Taiwan's Little Leaguers really that good? Were they that much better than kids from the good old U.S. of A? And even if you conceded that, yes, the Taiwanese were that good, there was another question which no one seemed to ask very loudly:

How come not one kid from Taiwan ever showed up later in the major leagues?

America's other professional sports—basketball, football, hockey, golf—have pulled in participants from all over the world. But of all those talented baseball kids from Taiwan and other Asian countries, not one ever got to the Bigs. How come?

The answer to that question would come tumbling out in the next couple of weeks. And it would involve a shameful Little League secret having to do with...

But wait. I am getting ahead of my story.

For now, let's go back to that bus barreling through the Susquehanna Valley toward Williamsport, Pennsylvania.

I have already mentioned one of the other adults with me, Denny Mayfield. Let me qualify that: Denny is actually an apprentice adult. He could be the poster boy for the Peter Pan Syndrome. The operator of a landscaping business, Denny, 44, is married and the father of one of our players.

Simply put, Denny loves games. He approaches sports the way Rommel approached the desert. Intensely.

When kids in our neighborhood play a ball game in the street, they usually do so in front of Denny's house. The reason is that Denny probably organized the game.

Denny could probably tell us how many stitches there are on a baseball. But I'm not sure he could tell you how many U.S. senators there are from California. His outlook is like that of the Sean Penn surfer character in "Fast Times at Ridgemont High," the one who says, "All I need in life to be happy is some cool brews and heavy waves."

Later in 1992, after the baseball season, I was honored at a luncheon given by my alma mater, Long Beach City College. Denny showed up wearing a suit. He had gone out and bought it for the occasion. That touched me deeply. His wife, Debbie, later told me it was the first suit he ever owned.

The third adult in our entourage was Larry Lewis, the team's manager. When not involved with Little League, Larry is a lawyer. Big time. He is a partner in one of Southern California's most prestigious firms: Allen, Matkins, Leck, Gamble and Mallory. At any given moment, Larry is carrying a killer caseload of court suits that involve millions and millions of dollars.

Denny and I attended the same Long Beach high school, Wilson, whose sports alumni include Bobby Grich, Andy Messersmith, Hall of Fame pitcher Bob Lemon, and former water polo star Jeff Losch, a good-looking guy who set local phone lines ablaze by returning to his 20-year reunion as a good-looking woman.

Larry had attended nearby Milliken High, where he'd been a halfback and had run the hundred-yard dash in under 10 seconds.

In those long-ago years at Wilson, Denny and I learned just about all one needs to know to get through life. Except one thing: No one taught us how to keep kids under control. We were probably the three weakest Little League disciplinarians in all of America. Having us chaperone kids across the U.S. was like having convicts transport other convicts.

The families and friends of the players were heading for Williamsport via other flights. But the kids, plus Larry, Denny and I, were flying on tickets supplied by Little League Baseball, Inc.

That raised a curious matter. Each U.S. team competing at the World Series has its airfare paid by Little League headquarters in Williamsport.

Also competing are four teams from countries outside the U.S. But the curious thing, we learned, was that Little League headquarters does not pay for the transportation of the international teams, although those teams travel the greatest distances to get to Pennsylvania. Those costs are borne by the individual countries. This is not an easy thing when the finalist team is from an impoverished, underdeveloped nation such as...well, such as the Philippines, one of the teams that, along with ours, had made it to the 1992 finals.

This is a bit amazing when you consider that Little League has a ton of bucks in its treasury (about $20 million, according to a report published just as we arrived in Williamsport). And since it makes money on the kids via TV game rights, you would think it would at least pay for the transportation of all players.

In short, it seemed to me that Little League was exploiting its visitors from abroad. That thought came back to me in the days ahead whenever I heard one of the Little League brass give an unctious speech that sounded as if the organization were run in pious partnership with God. In this case, of course, God being the junior partner.

As we were to find out, the Little League organization is also run with cold efficiency—by sweeping a ton or two of dirt under the rug when doing so suits official purposes.

A word about the members of our All-Star team: Although they were chosen from among six teams in Long Beach Little League, they too are from the same neighborhood as Larry, Denny and I. In fact, if you put the point of a compass on, say, Larry's house and drew a half-mile circle, it will embrace the homes of most of our players. I mention this because it became a significant factor in light of events that were about to unfold.

To earn the right to go to Williamsport, our guys won 17 consecutive baseball games. They did it with a lot of skill, a lot of laughs, and, to be honest, a bit of luck. On one occasion, winning a game even involved Larry's belly button. We may be the only team in baseball history with a game-winning navel.

Explanation: Larry has the grim distinction of possessing what is, undoubtedly, the ugliest navel in the hemisphere. It is the result of something that went awry—a surgical slip or some such thing. I cannot explain it precisely because, frankly, I have never wanted to know the details.

As proof of how really horrible it is, let me note that the kids love it. On a rare occasion or two, Larry has even been able to instill a few minutes of discipline by promising the urchins a sort of flasher's look at the button—provided they behave themselves.

The way his negative navel won us a game was as follows: We were behind in one contest, when shortstop-pitcher Alex DeFazio raised his doe eyes worshipfully toward Larry and spoke the most touching baseball words uttered by a kid since "Say it ain't so, Joe."

Said Alex, "Larry, if we win this one, will you show us your belly button?"

Larry agreed. The man is all heart (and navel). Word of the impending potential bonus swept through the dugout like electricity. We won that game by about 2,000 runs. Larry flashed the navel, and the kids squealed and shouted, "Oh, yuk! Oh, gross!"

Which, translated, means, "Wonderful!"

Amid a reverie of what I now think of as the Navel Game, I was drifting off at last to blessed sleep when the sudden braking of the bus jolted all of us awake.

Welcome to Williamsport.

We were in the place to which all Little League parents (well, at least 10 percent of them) dream of one day coming to see their kids compete for the world title.

In seasons past back in Long Beach, before our red-hot summer of 1992, Williamsport seemed to us as unreachable as Oz. It was the impossible dream.

But this middle-of-the-night arrival was the dream come true, I told myself as we stepped down from the bus. This was real. We were about to play in the Little League World Series.

(By definition, "Little League World Series" is used to designate all the games played during the week by the eight teams, and it is also used in reference to the final game played on Saturday between the U.S. and international champions.)

Standing in the Pennsylvania night, helping our groggy kids stagger off the bus, I never dreamed we were about to become embroiled in one of the most publicized sports scandals of 1992 and, most likely, the biggest scandal ever in the history of kids' sports. Before all that ran its course, the echoes would reverberate through two nations an ocean apart.

two

KEVIN MILLER

Height: 5'2"
Weight: 105

Filling in for the injured Dane Mayfield, Kevin hit his first home run of the all-star season—a three-run homer against San Ramon Valley in the 1992 Western Regional championship to help Long Beach win, 11–3. He batted .344.

Little League baseball is played in 74 countries, from Argentina to Zimbabwe.

It is played in Korea and Sri Lanka and among the mountains of Pakistan. In Belize and Ecuador and the islands of the Netherlands Antilles. In Norway and the Czech Republic and on the frozen earth of Mother Russia, where, as the now-departed Soviet commissars used to claim, the game was invented in Petrocooperstown, or some such place.

But for two years, 1992 and 1993, with an occasional lucky break, no kids in the world, in my biased opinion, played Little League baseball better than a handful of kids from Long Beach, California.

A city of almost 450,000 people lost in the shadow of Los Angeles, Long Beach is where I was born and raised. And it is where I returned in 1985, when my bat grew too heavy and my playing career in the major leagues came to an end.

The Long Beach Little League is made up of kids from the east side of the city. They play at a well-manicured field called Stearns Park, hard by the flight path of planes landing at Long Beach Airport. On lazy summer evenings, the Federal Express plane invariably roars by around the third or fourth inning.

I have been going to Stearns Park most of my life. A couple of centuries ago, I played Little League baseball there, aided by coaches whose patience and attention helped develop the skills that later got me to the big leagues.

In Little League World Series programs, it hurt me (without leaving deep psychological scars) to find my name not included in the list of big-leaguers, past and present, who also played in Little League. But the omission is minor compared to other gripes I have against the people at the top who run the Little League organization. We will get to those.

Back when I was nine, the Little League World Series was not on TV, as it is now. Nevertheless, all of us nine-year-olds knew about it—and knew that it was played in a place called Williamsport in a state called Pencil Something.

My own Little League seasons, in fact, were chock full of wistful thoughts about Williamsport. I never did get there, however. At least, not as a player.

Perhaps due to my influence, my family is a baseball family. The game is to us what chemicals are to the DuPonts.

My sons, Scott and Sean, have played Little League base-ball. My daughter, Shaelen, is active in Little League as a tee-baller. My wife, Deborah, manages Shaelen's tee-ball team.

(For those who do not know, tee-ball is a beginners' version of baseball for kids six and seven years old. There is no pitching in tee-ball. The batter hits the ball from a pedestal. That is, on those occasions when he or she actually manages to hit the ball.)

The 1985 season, which I played with the Toronto Blue Jays, was my last in the majors. At the end of their playing careers, some guys immediately start looking for another baseball niche, such as coaching or announcing. But I was not one of them.

Like Chico Escuela, the fictional retired Met on the old "Saturday Night Live," beisbol had been berry, berry good to ol' Jeff. But right then, I wanted nothing more than a vacation from the game in which I had spent my entire adult life up to that point. It was enough to be home again in Long Beach, to be away from the traveling, and to have time for family and friends.

One of those friends was Denny Mayfield, a pal from even before our days together at Wilson High School. In truth, I cannot remember a time in my life when Denny and I were not friends. We've probably known each other almost since we were born. At Wilson, we belonged to the same club, Athos. Back then, in the 1960s, there were high-school clubs that actually did good deeds. Athos was one of them. Most of us, Denny and I included, somehow managed to get our diplomas in those days without snorting coke or shooting our classmates.

When Denny got out of high school, as indicated earlier, he postponed adulthood because he was having so much fun with sports. Oh, sure, he was a responsible family man and all. But he was also having the time of his life coaching a tee-ball team in the nearby Los Altos Little League.

My sons, Scott and Sean, were playing for him. So was Denny's son, Dane. I went over to watch one day, and much as I enjoyed seeing my boys play, the real attraction was seeing Denny perform his magic with the kids.

They just loved him. He was a baseball Pied Piper. Denny could carry a bat and ball into a strange city, walk its length, and come out the other side with most of the city's kids following him. The only real difference between Denny and the Pied Piper is that, now and then, the Pied Piper probably got serious about life.

Although I thought it was too soon to jump back into any form of baseball, I must have gotten the bug from Denny that day. In retrospect, I'm glad. Had I not gotten the bug, I would have missed out on a lot of drama, trauma, heartache, confusion, worry and sleepless nights.

Plus the most fun I have ever had in my life.

I landed a gig coaching in what Little League calls its "Minors." The Minors, in which there are "A" and "B" divisions, consists of kids not yet ready for big-time Little League (or, as it is appropriately called, the "Majors").

After doing this a few seasons, I felt I had paid my dues and was ready to move up the Little League ladder. An expansion team was being added to our Major League division. I applied for the job of manager.

Such decisions go through the League's board of directors. The directors take this sort of thing very seriously, as if they were overseeing the Spanish Inquisition. In truth, however, they are usually glad to have anyone demented enough to volunteer to be a Little League manager. Or so I thought.

On the night the decision would be made, I went before the board and pleaded my case with, I thought, the eloquence of Daniel Webster. I noted my few seasons of Minor Little League experience, my 16 years of major-league experience, and even the fact that I had once been asked to throw out the first ball for a Little League season. The only other person who wanted the manager's job was a real estate broker named Steve Warshauer. After we made our cases, we were asked to step outside while the board voted.

Now, a former major leaguer going up against a real estate broker for the job of baseball manager is an unfair contest, and I felt sorry for Steve. I was on the verge of expressing my condolences when we were called back in to hear the voting results. As I suspected, the vote was not even close.

Steve won hands down.

I was dumbfounded. How could a real estate broker be chosen over a professional athlete, one whose baseball career had started in that very same Little League? I asked and was told they just thought Steve was more qualified. I did not buy that. There must have been another reason.

Later, I found out there was. The board was angy because, as a Minor League manager the previous year, I had failed to return the team's uniforms on time. Little League, I was to discover, is filled with people wanting nothing out of life except a pound of someone else's flesh. Besides, there was always the kick of telling people at cocktail parties, "Yeah, Jeff Burroughs. Most Valuable Player in the American League, 1974. I turned him down as Little League manager."

In truth, they had done me a great favor. Unable to manage, I landed a spot as a coach on a major team called the Pirates. The team's manager was a lawyer named Larry Lewis. Together, we would win, I think, as many games as any Little League manager and coach in America.

The Little League calendar begins with tryouts in January, which are followed by an event not unlike the gatherings of people who head Mafia families.

It is the Little League player draft.

I'm not sure how the draft is done in other Little League nations. In Germany, there may be a Little League Obergruppenbaseballmeister or some such figure who pounds the table, announces the rosters, and then releases all managers and coaches who swear their loyalty. In China—who knows? Maybe they just pick the players from right to left.

In the United States, however, the Little League draft is conducted like the NFL draft. Only much more seriously.

Managers and coaches, people whose drivers' licenses claim they are responsible adults, squeeze into someone's living room for hours, and scream, snarl, and otherwise behave like Woody Allen and Mia Farrow as they try to outdo each other in getting the best roster of players.

Does this surprise you? Did you think of Little League as a nicey-nice organization in which elves do the behind-the-scenes work and every kid who registers gets to play?

Well, part of that is true. Every kid does play. There are rules, as there should be, that require every kid to be put on a team and play in every game during the regular season. (In post-season, All-Star competition, however, in which a general spirit of throat-cutting prevails, the play-in-every-game rule is dropped.)

The player draft, to be sure, is not nicey-nice. The concept, as put forth by the star-gazers back in Williamsport, is that the draft will establish balance among teams in a league. But each manager wants to ensure that his team will be invincible. More league championships may be won in the draft than on the playing field.

With all that at stake, the draft is actually a display of domestic strife that ranks right up there with the American Civil War.

Never let a Little League manager from Long Beach (or any other place) tell you that team rosters do not matter to them. Or that having fun is the only thing that counts in Little League baseball. The truth is this: For every cherubic, rosy-cheeked Little Leaguer who takes to the field in Long Beach, there are probably two, three or more stories about how the adult managers and coaches fought tooth and nail to get him on their team.

Or, perhaps regrettably, fought tooth and nail to keep him off their team.

One year, the league inherited twins who had just moved from Upper Slovonia or some such place in Europe. There was a lot of maneuvering among managers to avoid getting the kids for two reasons. First, one of the kids had not even tried out and apparently had no interest in baseball. Second, his brother had tried out, was terrible, and had no knowledge of baseball. The latter fact became apparent when he went up to bat with his back turned toward the pitcher.

Yes, for all their shortcomings, they still wound up playing.

Okay, I admit it. The draft is a bit cruel. Things probably should not be that way at all in Little League. But things in fact are. And the ferocity of the draft is a big reason why Little League baseball is played better in some parts of the country than in others.

Smart managers and coaches (I like to think I'm one of them) start keeping records on the prowess of a neighborhood kid from about the time he or she first throws a rattle across the playpen. ("Hey, did you see that?")

Kids are being drafted who are 10, 11, and 12 years old. (Each team is limited to a maximum of eight 12-year-olds.) The process can be tricky. A good 10-year-old player, for example, may no longer be a good player by the time he or she reaches the doddering, ancient age of 12.

Also, you are drafting the kids into those levels of Little League baseball to which I referred earlier. They are, progressively, Minor B's, Minor A's and the Majors. Minor B and A divisions are sort of the farm system. The Majors are the kids who compete in the Little League World Series.

The first Little League draft in which I participated as a coach was a bit like the Olympics—if the Olympics had kicking, scratching, and clawing as categories.

It took place at the home of the league's vice president, Bob Skidmore. On arriving, I was told that I was not allowed to take part in the draft. There was some argument, but I had acquired new enemies who suggested immediately that I go home, a message that was underscored by having the door closed in my face.

Still, I was not without friends. One of them, Mike Tracy, told me to go home and call him every 10 minutes on his cellular phone. We could confer on who we should take in each round.

For a few rounds of the draft, this worked well. But then, during one conversation, I heard someone's voice say, "Quick! Take the telephone away! That's illegal!"

Mike suddenly said, "I have to go..." The phone went dead. It was like that moment in the movies when the resistance fighter is captured by the Gestapo.

The rest of the draft was mostly uneventful, save for one situation in which one father drafted another father's son, and a fistfight nearly erupted between them.

The fact that they were brothers-in-law was, apparently, immaterial when it came to the draft.

Part of the draft was to get to know as much about a player off the field as possible. Is the kid willing to play baseball four days a week? Is the kid's family planning to move within the next couple of years? Are the parents apt to get divorced? (Okay, that's pretty rough, but in truth a child caught in the middle of a custody fight can be a disrupting influence on an entire team.)

Before each draft, Larry Lewis, who has more nerve than a junk-bond salesman, would call parents and do interviews, asking all sorts of questions that were really none of his business. In the middle of one such inquiry, a mom named Wendy Hayes asked if she was being interviewed for a position with the Central Intelligence Agency.

Until the rule was changed a few years ago, it was possible to draft nine-year-olds into the Majors division of Little League. But hardly anyone wanted to waste a draft choice on a kid that young.

I became an exception.

In my first draft as a coach, in 1990, I was enamored with a pair of nine-year olds, the Miller twins—Chris and Kevin. Most of what I knew about them came not from baseball, but from seeing them on the soccer field, where they were awesome. At that age, a kid who can play soccer well can probably play baseball just as well. I wanted the Miller twins the way Donald Trump wanted Atlantic City.

I convinced Larry Lewis. On about the fifth round of the draft, when our manager's turn came, he said quietly, "Numbers 922 and 923, Chris and Kevin Miller."

You would have thought we had drafted a pair of dachshunds. The others laughed themselves silly. "Are you guys crazy? What are you trying to do?" Larry just smiled and said, "I think they can play ball."

What we were trying to do was build a team for the future; a dynasty, if you will. In Little League, there is not a lot of dynasty-building. Boys and girls have relatively short baseball careers before they get interested in other things, such as girls and boys.

But I felt pretty smug about it, sort of the way Jacob Rupert must have felt while assembling the 1927 Yankees.

As it turned out, on the playing field, the Miller twins were in over their heads that first year. But by the time they were 11—oh, my! They became two of the four kids who would play on both our 1992 and 1993 world championship teams.

In other respects, the twins were older than their years. By the time we came to the 1992 season, Kevin Miller had somehow picked up the ability to swear like a sailor's parrot. His parents are such well-mannered people that we could only marvel at this. It was as if he had read the Watergate transcripts before the expletives were deleted.

Now and then during a game, we would take him aside, and say, "Kevin, you can get thrown out of a game for that. You can't say those things in Little League. Church, maybe, but not Little League."

Another of the kids who would play on both teams was nine-year-old Sean Burroughs, my son. (The draft is conducted in such a way that managers and coaches are usually able to have their own kids on their teams.)

We phoned Pat Miller to tell her that her boys had been drafted. This was a bit perilous. Telling a mom that her nine-year-old has been drafted to play alongside 12-year-olds is a bit like saying he has just been drafted by the Green Bay Packers or a small Third-World army. (Even my own parents would not let me play in the Little League Majors at age 10.)

Pat was pretty upset.

But Al, her husband, simply shrugged, and said, "Sounds good to me. If the kids want to play, let them."

One manager involved in that draft recognized exactly what we were trying to do. He was a savvy guy named Al Huntley, who has been a Little League manager since about the time Napoleon retreated from Moscow.

As soon as he heard us draft the Millers, Al took out his notebook, which is loaded with meticulous information on players—little entries such as, "Can't hit slider thrown on 3-and-2 count by freckle-faced lefthander when barometer is rising." Al thumbed through his book looking at data he had compiled on nine-year-olds. He was not going to be caught short if, in a couple of years, the Miller twins turned out to be a pair of Henry Aarons.

He picked a nine-year-old named Alex DeFazio, who was about the size of a loaf of bread. Now the others in the room thought Al was crazy, too. But Alex also wound up playing on both those world championship teams.

I had seen Alex at a December 1989 baseball camp run by former Pittsburgh Pirate pitcher Vern Ruhle. By the time most kids in our neighborhood are eight or nine, they have been playing baseball or tee-ball for four or five years. But Alex had never played. The day I saw him in that camp was his very first day of baseball.

In the batting cages, he did not have a clue as to what he was doing. It would have been laughable, even pathetic, except for two things. First, he had a great swing. Second, for all the things he did wrong, he still managed to hit the ball most of the time. It was astonishing.

Alex, in fact, is an inspiring story. He was born with a heart irregularity called aortic stenosis. Essentially, his heart valve does not always close completely.

It is a malady that occurs once in every umpteen hundred thousand births. Yet, quite amazingly, Larry Lewis has the same condition. A few years ago, while in his 30s, Larry had a pig valve inserted in his heart.

Although the condition does not prevent a kid from participating in organized sports, Alex was vying to become a world-class skateboarder instead. His parents, Tony and Candy, the latter another of my old schoolmates from Wilson, laid down the law: "Get involved in a sport—

any sport—for one year. Then, if you want to throw your life away on the skateboard, you can do so."

Alex chose baseball, and he went off to that instructional camp as if he had been ordered into the jaws of hell. But he fell in love with the game. And later he became a top-notch athlete in other sports, including surfing and skateboarding, in which he has tremendous coordination and balance.

He wound up playing four seasons of great Little League baseball, and he stayed about the size of a fire hydrant. Along the way, he picked up a great nickname: "The Toy Cannon."

Alex proved something. If you have a big heart, even one with aortic stenosis, you don't have to be a big person to play great baseball.

three

CHRIS MILLER

Height: 5'0"
Weight: 95

The left-handed version of his twin brother, Kevin. Good hitter. On his regular-season Pirates team, he belted two home runs in the Tournament of Champions in June. Chris served as a pinch hitter on the all-star team.

When I am not involved with baseball, look for me in the ocean. Or, more precisely, above the ocean.

I am a fishing fanatic, and I do most of my fishing in salt water. I enjoy it so much that I have become an amateur marine biologist. The undersea world I study is, perhaps, the most competitive world there is—except for Congress and the used-car business.

You eat something or it eats you. It's that simple.

In your world and mine, competition is not quite that keen, but it is still an important factor in our lives. As a coach in Little League (and, in the off-season, on the soccer field), I feel part of my job is to prepare kids to face the competitive world that awaits them when they become adults.

Sure, there is nothing wrong with having fun on the Little League field. But neither is there anything wrong with a manager or coach instilling a little competitive spirit. And that brings me to the sometimes touchy subject of competitive sports among young people.

Yes, I know. You did not buy this book because you are a psychology major. Nor did you buy it to become more competitive than your neighbor or boss. You bought it to read the story of how a team of Dennis the Menaces from Long Beach, California, managed to win back-to-back world championships, a feat accomplished by no other U.S. team in the history of Little League.

Okay, I will tell you that story. You will get your money's worth.

But trust me, as the politicians say. In order to better understand how our little guys triumphed over thousands of other little guys (or sometimes not so little, as we shall see), I need to set the scene by telling you a bit about my approach to dealing with kids.

Keep in mind that Benjamin Spock Burroughs is not talking about how to raise kids. As a child expert and baby-sitter, I am Class D. I am talking strictly about how to deal with kids on the baseball field. For off-the-field advice, consult the real Spock (the one without the funny ears) or my sidekick in life, Deborah Burroughs.

Little League managers and coaches are often criticized for being too intense, for putting too much pressure on the kids. Some of that is valid criticism. I've seen managers strut and shout as if they were preparing their kids to march into Poland, and I've seen coaches who probably keep horsewhips in their equipment bags.

But for every bad guy at a Little League helm, there are bunches of good guys, coaches and managers. Hardly any of them are baseball experts. They are simply good men—and, increasingly, women—who give a lot of time unselfishly to help keep kids out of trouble. Most of these good folks take a lot of sass from parents who could not do half as well as managers or coaches.

Mind you, I have no problem with parents who stick up for their kids. But I have problems with parents who think their kids are better than the other kids. Or parents who have a lot to say about what is happening on the field—without knowing why it is happening.

It is not unusual for a parent who has missed, say, the first five games of a season to show up at the sixth and question the batting order or wonder why his or her kid is not pitching or in the starting line-up.

A few of those parents may even think something like, "Look at Jeff, the fascist. He's not in this for the kids. He's in it for himself. He wants to win more than the kids want to win. He puts too much pressure on them."

Let's talk about that. About pressure and about teaching kids to win.

There will always be a few parents, I suppose, who think winning is not important. Or, even worse, that there is something inexcusable or psychologically wrong about teaching kids to win.

Baloney!

First, let's look at pressure. Applied to young kids in sports, pressure does not work. It is non-productive. No caring, competent manager or coach will pressure his team. To get a kid to play baseball well, you must treat him well. You must support him as much as you can. You can't constantly get on him for mistakes.

On our way to winning those two world championships, Larry Lewis and I never yelled at our guys. (Off the field, when they were misbehaving, we probably didn't yell at them enough.) They knew that if they went up to bat or went out to pitch and failed, we would not scream at them when they came back to the dugout. We simply tried to sit them down and explain what they should have done.

Consequently, our kids never felt that if they failed, they would get in trouble. As a result, they succeeded a lot more than they failed.

I have seen Little League managers who do use pressure, who say such things as, "Johnny, we expect you to carry our team." Or "Don't forget, we drafted you in the first round." They'll chew a kid out for making an error or swinging at a bad pitch.

What's the point of that? I've never seen a kid yet who wanted to strike out or make an error. In the majors, I struck out 1,135 times. But I guarantee you, not once was I trying to do it.

So why put unnecessary pressure on a kid? Almost always, the kid is the first one to realize he did not do well. When one of our guys struck out or dropped a ball, Larry and I always made it a practice to say, "Don't worry about it. You'll get it right the next time."

As for winning, I have no reluctance about emphasizing it. After all, winning is what sports are all about. Winning is what life is all about. Putting your child on a team in which no thought is given to winning is as silly as sending him to a college in which no thought is given to academic success.

Furthermore, kids are naturally competitive. The ones I get in Little League have been competitive since they were about five years old. Most of their parents are competitive, too, although some don't admit it, and a few even deny it. But try coaching one game in which the parents don't think you want to win. You'll be lucky after the game if they don't do funny things to your tires or hang you in the town square.

Kids want to win, too. They watch what's going on. And they watch you, as their manager or coach. If they think you aren't trying to win, they'll wonder what's wrong with you. Those fuzzy-headed sociologists who think kids do not want to win have not done their research. Yes, playing games is fun. But winning them is even more fun.

Once in a while, I run into a parent who is offended by the fact that I stress winning to the kids. I don't understand that attitude. How do they expect to prepare their kids for the real world? Little League, and any sport for young people, should have two purposes: 1. To have fun. 2. To get kids ready for real life.

Bear with me. Let me share a couple more thoughts on the psychology of kids' sports before getting on with the story of "The Little Team That Could."

(The title, by the way, comes from a headline written by John Woolard, a copy editor for the *Long Beach Press-Telegram*. Thank you, John.)

First, in the quest to win, there must be guidelines. You have to stress winning without overdoing it, without letting kids become consumed by it. And you cannot stress it so much that when the kids lose, they are overwhelmed to the point of being unable to function.

Second, you have to keep the level of frustration down. Frustration is often a factor in Little League baseball, as it is in big league baseball. Among the little guys it sometimes erupts into tears. Anyone watching the Little League World Series on television is almost certain to see a kid cry—invariably, a kid from the losing team.

Champions or not, our team was no different. We left a few puddles along the road to Williamsport.

This is to be expected. At 11 and 12, the ages of Little League World Series competitors, kids are pretty sensitive. Probably half our guys cried at one point or another. It was not because they were sissies. In fact, it was often because they were incredibly intense. Or, on occasion, frustrated.

A couple of our kids—Jeff Warshauer and Kevin Sullivan come to mind—were prone to cry. They are very competitive kids. Kevin, in fact, may have tried harder at baseball than anyone on our team.

I can accept the crying now and then, but when a kid gets so intense or frustrated that he cries every time things do not go right, that kid might be better off playing another sport.

Besides, you just never know when things will turn around. Tomorrow or the next day, there might not be anything to cry about. Tomorrow or the next day, a kid might hit a homer and suddenly be the happiest boy in America.

It really rips me up to see a kid cry. It makes me sad. It makes me feel I haven't done something right. But when it happens, you have to hope the kid has enough confidence in you to listen to what you tell him.

What do you tell a kid who gets down on himself? You have to make him understand that it is not the end of the world if something goes wrong. That sounds pretty simplistic, but it's amazing how many kids are never told anything like that. They're the ones who are apt to cry the minute their coaches yell at them. Under those circumstances, crying exacerbates a bad situation, and things go downhill from there.

Let me add to this a few words about parents, and about how they impact on kids' sports.

Most kids mirror their parents. When a parent's attitude is, "Yeah, I want to win, but it's more important that my kid has a good time," the kid will reflect that, too. More significantly—and more negatively—if the parents are out of control, so are the kids.

A loose-cannon parent, one who is out of control, is a Little League coach's nightmare. (Unless the coach is also out of control, which happens.) One such parent—breeding discontent, spreading rumors, gossiping maliciously—can spread like a cancer throughout the stands. Meanwhile, the parent's kid is likely to be doing the same among the team.

Our 1992 and 1993 All-Star teams were lucky. Like most Little League managers and coaches, we had our share of disputes with parents, to be sure. But not once did we have a parent who came remotely close to being out of control. That's one of the reasons we won.

Sure, we had misunderstandings and disagreements. One that stands out in memory resulted from the fact that our practice sessions were pretty intense. We tried to make them fun (usually by dividing the team and having a game), but they sometimes got rough. Parents did not always appreciate the intensity of our training.

After one practice session, a team dad came at me full of demons because his son had been hit in the head with a pitch. Since I hope to continue living in Long Beach after this book is published, let's call this guy Dad X. And his son Egbert X.

Other managers and coaches who had Egbert on their Little League or soccer teams had known rocky moments with Dad X. He typified the kind of parent who thinks his kid can do no wrong. You know the type. If his son held up a bank, it would somehow be the bank's fault.

During practice sessions, Dad X would hang around the field more than I think a parent should. There is, after all, a point at which parents must display some trust in the manager and coach.

Further, when Egbert did not do well at practice, Dad X was inclined to say such things as, "The pitcher is throwing too hard. He's not letting Egbert hit the ball."

Larry or I would explain, "To tell you the truth, we are not trying to let Egbert hit the ball. We are trying our very best to strike Egbert out. That is what pitchers do in baseball. They try to strike batters out. We are trying to do the same. This is how kids learn."

I do not like any kid to get hit in the head, but if there was one kid on the team I especially did not want to get hit in the head, it was Egbert. I knew his father would protest such a mishap to the maximum.

On this particular day, Chad Stuart, the older brother of one of our players and a fine baseball player himself, was throwing batting practice. He unleashed one that caught Egbert on the noggin. (Yes, he had his helmet on.)

Egbert decided Chad had deliberately tried to hit him, a notion he undoubtedly developed from inheriting his father's genes. He reported this, in tears, to Dad X. The elder X sought me out, and lectured me in the kind of tone used by someone delivering a speech to the Republican National Convention.

He said, "Please tell that guy not to hit Egbert in the head. He's all scared and everything."

I looked X in the eye and said in measured words, "Chad is not trying to hit Egbert in the head. Chad likes Egbert very much. But Chad is not a machine. He is a human being, and every now and then he does throw a wild pitch."

I don't think X bought a word of it. In fact, it would not surprise me if he concluded that the entire Little League organization had been established throughout the United States and many other parts of the world so that, on a certain day in 1992, someone could hit Egbert in the head with a baseball.

Being a dad myself, I understand all this. In a reverse situation, I might have behaved somewhat like Dad X myself. When you get down to it, we're all just Papa and Mama Bears, trying to protect our cubs.

Finally, I recall one dad who was savage in his competitiveness. He would have done almost anything to win. But when his son's team was getting beat one day, 21 to 1, suddenly the guy was screaming, "That's OK, kids. The score is not important. Just have fun."

He ordered his son to bat from the opposite side of the plate, throw with his opposite hand, and, in general, goof around. This was a guy who, earlier in the year, had threatened to punch the manager for not pitching his son.

If parents do not drive managers or coaches crazy, an occasional league official often will. Like the one who drove Larry to paranoia during the regular season.

This particular official had the job of drawing up the regular season schedule. Larry, as manager of the Pirates, somehow convinced himself that the schedule was designed to put his team at a disadvantage. To prove his point in best lawyer tradition, Larry and his secretary prepared the most complicated chart ever made outside a nuclear physics lab.

Along with the chart, Larry delivered what he thought was an absolutely devastating presentation on alleged conspiracy and corruption in Little League game scheduling. It was hilarious. And a bit like watching a Desert Storm briefing by General Norman Schwarzkopf.

Not a single change was made in the schedule.

Now, enough about parents, psychology and paranoia. Let's start down the the road to Williamsport.

four

ALI STRAIN-BAY

Height: 5'3"
Weight: 100

A two-time all-star, the third
baseman-outfielder smacked a
two-run homer against San Ramon
Valley in the Western Regionals.
He led the regular-season Angels
in hitting and batted .297 as an
all-star. Ali was a terrific defensive
player.

One of the recurring sentences in this book will be: "I let
Larry handle it."

This phrase is crucial to our story. It is the key to
understanding how Larry and I worked together as manager and coach.

Essentially, my job was to teach baseball. Essentially, Larry's job was to be in charge of administrative matters, provide line-ups to umpires, placate angry parents,
duel with officials in Williamsport, process death threats,
pay bills, deliver inspirational speeches to supporters, protect us in times of natural disaster, and represent us at the
World Court in The Hague.

It was a fair division of responsibility. After all, the
man is a lawyer.

When our 1992 season ended in late May, the Pirates, the team Larry managed and I coached, were champions of the Long Beach Little League. The next event on the calendar was the selection of an All-Star team to compete against the All-Stars of other leagues. Being the manager and coach of the league champs meant that Larry and I would pilot the All-Star team, just as we had done the year before.

All-Star selection is where the road to Williamsport really begins. And to get to Williamsport, all a kid has to do is:

1. Play brilliantly during the regular season.

2. Play so brilliantly as to be chosen for his league's All-Star team.

3. Compete as part of his team against the All-Star teams of other Little Leagues.

4. Make sure his team defeats all the All-Star teams in the district, then in the section (made up of several districts), then in the division (for us, just about all of Southern California), then all the top All-Star teams from the western United States.

The odds of his getting to Pennsylvania are about 7,200 to 1, since 7,200 is the estimated number of Little League All-Star teams in the world.

Or the odds against *her* getting to Pennsylvania. A few years ago, a team from nearby San Pedro, California, made it to Williamsport with a girl playing first base. That apparently caused all kinds of complications at the Williamsport compound where the teams are housed. She had to be put up at a local hotel.

As you can guess from the odds posted above, no one at this early stage was making hotel reservations in

Williamsport. Yet, each spring in Little League, a young boy's fancy turns to Pennsylvania—as do the fancies of his parents, grandparents, neighbors, coach and manager.

From day one, you think about Williamsport sort of harmlessly, the way you might think about playing lead guitar for the Rolling Stones or sinking a 40-foot putt to win the U.S. Open.

From day two, you get serious about it.

Each All-Star team has 14 members. Twelve are elected by the league's players. They cannot vote for anyone on their own team, and they can only vote for kids 11 and 12 years old.

On the surface, that sounds like a popularity contest, but it is a surprisingly good electoral system. Kids may be more responsible voters than adults. In Little League, at least, they are pretty consistent about picking the best players over those who might be the most popular. And they handle the selection much better than their parents would. If parents picked All-Star players, you would hear the screaming matches and teeth-gnashing from here to Patagonia. Wherever Patagonia is.

After the kids vote, two more players are chosen by the manager and coach. Even that seemingly innocuous task has the potential to pit neighbor against neighbor, invoke civil uprisings, and turn rivers to blood.

Let me give you an example. It involves John and Linda Beaver and their son, Ryan. John and Linda have long been friends with Larry's family and mine. Ryan was a fine Little Leaguer who, later in 1992, would play a crucial role for us in Williamsport.

But back in 1991, Ryan was not chosen for the All-Star team. His parents had been banking that he would be chosen. This meant someone had to break the news to John and Linda, who, when it comes to their kids, can be pretty volatile people. Telling them Ryan did not make All-Stars was akin to telling Fidel Castro that the sugar crop had failed.

I let Larry handle it.

He dropped in on John and Linda, intending to stay a couple of minutes and break the news casually. What he said was something like, "Hey, guys, how ya doin'? Great day today. And by the way, Ryan did not make the All-Star team."

All hell broke loose. By the time Larry left their house, nearly a broken man, entire new republics had been formed. Generations of small animals had come and gone.

John screamed at Larry. Linda screamed at Larry. John and Linda cried at Larry. There is no telling what might have happened were it not for the fact that they were best friends.

For a week or so, John did not talk to me. Then it was discovered that one player chosen for the All-Star team was not eligible. Records showed that he lived outside the district. It was only a few yards outside the district, but our league was tough in policing such offenses. (Later, we ran up against cases involving foreign Little League players who lived hundreds of miles outside their districts.)

When the kid was declared ineligible by virtue of a few yards, there was a sudden vacancy on the All-Star team. It was up to Larry and me to fill it. Our list of candidates included Ryan Beaver, who really was a fine player. We chose him. And possibly saved a couple of lives. Larry's and mine.

After Ryan was chosen, I stopped driving past the Beavers' house at 90 miles an hour.

Ryan turned out to be a great acquisition. In addition to his ability as a player, he had a fascinating bit of body language in which his arms would suddenly rise slowly, then jut out from his sides. He usually did this to shrug off an error or other mishap.

Combined with a silly look on his face, the effect was that of looking like the world's largest chicken. The other kids loved it.

The only thing tougher than telling a parent that his child did not make the All-Star team is telling a parent that his child DID make the All-Star team.

Really. It takes a lot of guts to phone a parent who has sat (often suffered) through dozens of regular-season Little League games and break the news that they will now be able to sit through another dozen games and, at the same time, abandon their vacation plans (not to mention their hotel deposit) on Maui.

I let Larry handle that.

One of the boys the players chose for our 1992 All-Stars was a kid named Eric Powell. During the regular season, he had played for Steve Warshauer. Eric was a fine player, but there was great confusion about where he lived. He seemed to have more addresses than George Bush. Eventually, we got it all straightened out, and Eric was cleared to play on the team.

But just before our first All-Star tournament, Eric's father told me, "As soon as the tournament ends, we'll be taking off with Eric." They were going east on vacation.

I blinked at him in disbelief. It meant that if we did win the first tournament, Eric would not be with us for other tournaments. It was like Pop Ruth telling Miller Huggins to forget the rest of the Yankee season because Pop was taking Babe on vacation.

Our only choice was to drop Eric from the team.

Funny thing is, I never again saw Eric or his father. Maybe they moved. But I always wondered what they felt upon realizing that little family vacation cost Eric the experience of playing in the Little League World Series.

We scrambled to fill that vacancy. There were six or seven kids who were pretty close in ability and attitude. Any one of them could have been on the team. We couldn't decide who the 14th player should be, and it got to the point that we were about to flip a coin or light incense to the gods of All-Stars.

By then, the other 13 All-Stars had been practicing together. They were starting to jell as a team, and the chemistry among them was really terrific. So we did an odd little thing. We simply did not fill the vacancy.

It should be noted that in this era of political correctness, we had assembled a mostly white team. That could not be helped. It reflected the league, and the league reflected the neighborhood in East Long Beach from which the players were drawn. It was a predominantly white area, with only a few African-Americans and Hispanics.

This came up in a discussion later in the year. The All-Star season had ended, and one day I was in Phil Trani's, a Long Beach restaurant and watering hole popular with sports people.

By then, of course, the All-Stars had gotten a ton of publicity, and their faces were fairly well-known, at least in Long Beach.

A rough-looking guy came up to me at Trani's and began talking about the team. I didn't know him personally, but he was a former boxer and the father of a locally prominent boxer. The guy was black, and in the middle of our conversation about Little League, he suddenly hit me with, "You don't have any minorities on the All-Stars, do you?"

Deciding to banter a bit, I countered with, "Well, now, let me see. To tell you the truth, I haven't really thought about it. Let me take a minute and think because I don't really look at my kids as minorities, but just as my Little League team."

He said, "Yeah, sure. You guys didn't have any minorities in the whole league either."

Actually, we did. We had several black and Latino players. But, in truth, I'm not big on all this nose-counting stuff that goes on these days to see if an acceptable number from each group is represented. I especially do not like it when kids are involved. They don't look at other kids as white, black, Mexican or whatever. Adults teach them to do that. The grown-ups come along, start counting noses, start protesting, and get the kids get all screwed up.

Anyway, I let this guy push me a bit more about minorities on the All-Stars until, finally, I said, "Wait! It's coming back to me now. Yes. We did have one African-American, until his family decided to take him on vacation and pull him off the team." I was referring, of course, to Eric Powell.

By now, the guy was looking at me as if I were the Grand Kleagle of the Klan. Then I hit him with it.

I reminded him that we had Ali.

It seemed that Ali Strain-Bay had been in our Little League forever. He started on my tee-ball team. We drafted him up to the Minor B's, then Minor A's. Al Huntley drafted him onto his Major League team. Ali's brother, Ira, a year older, also was a whale of a player. I used to think of Ira as "Mr. Little League," although he hardly ever said a word.

Infield or outfield, Ali was a great defensive player. But a freak thing happened to him at the bat after he made All-Stars. He had a streak of seven at-bats in which he got hit by pitches five times. As might happen to any-one, the experience left him pretty ball-shy. After a while, the pitcher would be winding up, and Ali would be jumping for the dugout.

But what a kid. Ali, whose real name is Ismael, just dug in there and got his hits—even though he was scared to death in the batter's box. That's the mark of real guts: to hang in there when you're scared.

Before we got into All-Star play, a sad thing occurred.

Later, I will have something to say about umpires, and about how the quality of umpiring now and then gets pretty terrible in Little League. One delightful exception to that, however, was a great guy named Ruben Gutierrez, who had been chief umpire of the Long Beach Little League for nine years.

Weighing less than three pounds when he was born, Ruben literally spent his first days in a shoebox. He was still a baby when he contracted polio. That kept him from competing later in sports, but it did not keep him from umpiring, coaching and working full-time as a school playground aide in nearby Lynwood.

Ruben loved to talk to kids. Even while umpiring behind the plate, he was always chatting with the catcher or batter.

He was pretty gifted at persuading kids to stay in school and/or stay away from gangs. At school, when he caught a kid doing something wrong, he talked to the lad instead of sending him to the principal. The kids loved him for that. Our Little League kids loved him, too.

One of Ruben's most ardent fans on our team was Ryan Stuart. Ryan had hit a couple of homers in one game, and Ruben had managed to retrieve the balls. At the end of the game, he gave one ball to Ryan and, for some reason, Ruben said he would give him the other the next time he saw him.

There was no next time. On the night of June 17, 1992, after umpiring a game, Ruben was heading home when his car was struck by another. It was a hit-and-run. (The driver of the other car was later arrested.) Ruben, who was not wearing a seat belt, was killed instantly. He was 42 years old.

In death, Ruben became a part of the team, as you will see. So much a part that his memory seemed even to give us an extra edge. We called it "The Ruben Factor."

For the rest of the All-Star season, we wore "R.G." armbands.

five

KEVIN SULLIVAN

Height: 5'6"
Weight: 135

One of the top hitters on the team.
Kevin came through with clutch
hitting when it was needed most.
He hit his first home run, a
three-run shot, on his birthday
against San Ramon Valley in the
Western Regional Championship
game. In 1992 this left fielder
batted .344, had 11 RBI's and
scored eight times.

One of the two kids Larry and I originally chose for the team was a quiet guy named David Gonzalez. His mother and father, Fernando and Jean, were strict parents, but very supportive of their kids.

Throughout the All-Star season, David was plagued by a sore arm. As a result, he didn't get to play all that much—and certainly not as much as Fernando thought he should be playing. All this came to a head one day in a rather classic parent-coach Little League confrontation.

When the All-Star team was chosen, we tried to explain to parents that, unlike the regular season, their kids would not necessarily start in every game or play all six innings, which is the length of Little League games. Evidently, Fernando did not get the word.

By the time of the incident, we had won our first tournament, the district tournament, with five consecutive victories. And we had advanced to the next level, the section play-offs.

(We were only the second team in the four decades of Long Beach Little League to win the district title. The first team had been the previous year's All-Stars, also coached by Larry and me.)

After a section game in which David only got to bat once, I was still in the dugout when Denny Mayfield whispered, "Watch out. Here comes Fernando, and he's really on the warpath."

Indeed he was. Nostrils flaring, he stormed into the dugout.

"David isn't on the team any more," he said.

I asked why.

"He isn't playing enough. In one game, we were up by a couple of hundred runs or something, and David only got one at-bat before you took him out of the game."

Now, some people may have a different opinion of me, but I happen to know I am a wonderful, placid guy who does not have an ounce of malice in his heart and who is probably in line for the Nobel Peace Prize. But when a parent accuses me of some kind of conspiracy not to play his kid, my peacenik machinery goes haywire.

I got even angrier than Fernando. We started yelling at each other and were soon engaged in one of those incredibly brilliant screaming exchanges that people get into.

"Don't you scream at me!"

"Who's screaming?"

"You're screaming."

"Yeah, well, I'll scream if I want to."

And so on.

Amid the screaming, I somehow reminded Fernando that David had not been voted on the All-Stars by the kids, but had been picked by Larry and me.

"Don't get mad at me," I said. "If it weren't for me, David would not be on the team."

That did it. Fernando grabbed David, and said, "Let's go." Good kid that he is, David was going to do whatever his father wanted. They walked off together.

Then Fernando, turned, came back, and threw down the glove David had been using. "You can have your glove back," he said.

I had no idea what he was talking about. But when I looked down, I realized it was a glove of mine that I had given to David two years earlier.

There is a little voice inside me that always has to have the last word. As Fernando departed again, I shouted, "Well, you could at least thank me for letting David use my glove the last two years."

It is sometimes astonishing how small-minded a nice guy like me can be.

I felt terrible for David. And terrible for me since this meant we had another sudden vacancy on the team. It was a minor crisis. And I did what I always do in a crisis, minor or otherwise.

I let Larry handle it.

"Hey, Larry. Why don't you let Fernando cool off overnight. Then give him a call tomorrow and use your best lawyer-ese on the guy. David's a good player. We need him."

So Larry called the next morning and found Fernando disgruntled as a head-hunter.

"Got a minute?" Larry asked. Fernando snapped, "Hurry up! I don't have time for you guys." It was not the sort of beginning that promised successful negotiations.

But Mr. Manager-Lawyer pleaded the case. And when Fernando finally settled down, Larry said, "Why don't you ask David if he wants to play on the team?"

Fernando did precisely that. David wanted to play. There was no more trouble from Fernando.

One of the joys of getting to Williamsport later that summer was seeing Fernando in the stands.

Now, and then, Fernando's genes came to the fore in David. We loved the kid, but we learned that if he were pushed too far, he would come at you just like his dad.

Denny Mayfield was one of several Little League managers and coaches helping the All-Stars practice between games. At one practice session, he took to ribbing David by calling him a name.

David took offense. He came up to about Denny's belt buckle, but that did not stop him from lacing into Denny. "Don't you ever call me that," he shouted.

Denny started laughing. In turn, David did the only thing he could think to do to emphasize his point. He threw his bat at Denny.

Well, Denny hopped out of the way of the bat and laughed all the more. Next thing I knew, David was laughing, too. That was the end of that.

In retrospect, David had the best time of anyone on that 1992 All-Star team. Suddenly, he wasn't a quiet kid anymore. He really came out of his shell. By the end of the summer, we couldn't shut him up.

He had an especially good time at the western regional tournament in San Bernadino. There was a swimming pool there for the players, and every time I turned around, David would be saying, "Hey, Jeff, can I go in the pool now?" I'd say, "Sure, have a good time."

Later, I found out he couldn't swim.

The millions of you who are keeping notes as you read this book will probably want a summary of how the kids were deployed on the field.

Since we moved them from position to position a lot, there was really no hard and fast line-up. But as individuals, they played the following positions:

Ryan Beaver: Pitcher, third base, shortstop.
Sean Burroughs: Pitcher, shortstop.
Alex DeFazio: Second base, center field.
David Gonzalez: Third base.
Michael Holden: Right field.
Dane Mayfield: Pitcher, right field.
Chris Miller: Second base.
Kevin Miller: Left field.
Randall Shelley: Center field, pitcher,
Ali Strain-Bay: Third base, right field.
Ryan Stuart: First base.
Kevin Sullivan: Left field.
Jeff Warshauer: Catcher.

Everything that could help us win was considered and, in most cases, put into use. This even included something the parents called "Sure-to-Win Oil," a balm that, according to rumor, had been purchased in a witchcraft store and was said to have been produced from eye of something and liver of something else and so on.

It was applied to players here and there until a couple of conservative parents objected. Had there been enough time for me to document that it really worked, we might have bought a six-pack of the stuff.

We won the section tournament (three wins, no losses) and moved on to the division level, consisting of teams from most of Southern California. Our club was rolling. It was as if the kids wanted to impress Larry and me. And impress each other. They wanted to show they were macho guys, and they kept reaching deep within themselves to achieve new heights.

Every day became a challenge to see if they could make themselves better than the previous day. And I do mean every day. We were practicing or playing without days off.

Our approach to practice was different from most teams, which helps account for the fact that we kept winning while other teams were falling by the Little League wayside.

We practiced "before the fact." That is to say, we practiced in a way that anticipated the mistakes a kid could be expected to make on the field. You can't wait until the middle of a game for a kid to make a mistake, then go out on the field and say, "No, this is the way you should have done it." Yet a surprising number of Little League managers and coaches do precisely that.

For all our success, however, problems continued to crop up. There was, for example, a phone call from Mike Sullivan, whose boy, Kevin, was one of the most determined players on our team.

Mike was the kind of parent who is so dedicated that he thinks he is to blame for every little thing that goes wrong with his youngster.

His call came at a time when Kevin was not playing well defensively and, consequently, was not getting into every game. Mike took it personally, as if he and his wife, Nancy, were responsible.

"I'd like to know what we've been doing wrong," he said.

I assured him they had not done anything wrong and told him, "To be honest, right now I think Kevin Miller is a better defensive player than your son. I know the team can score runs, but I want us to field the best defensive team we can. If your boy shows improvement defensively, he'll be in there."

It was as if I had said all that to my dog. Mike heard none of it. "Yeah," he said, "but I really want to know what we did wrong. Did we do something wrong somewhere?"

For what it's worth, Kevin Sullivan became a great defensive player, and in Williamsport he made an absolutely impossible catch that saved a game.

When we were not having trouble with parents, it seemed we were having trouble with umpires. In one game, for example, we got into a tangle with an ump over a teensy piece of paper that is known as the "NOCSEA seal."

Most likely, I will go to my grave without ever knowing what the acronym means, but before a piece of equipment can be used in a Little League game, it must have the NOCSEA seal of approval. Presumably, that means the equipment has passed some kind of inspection and that it is safe for the little codgers to use.

The rule does not say much for the rank-and-file managers and coaches. In fact, it suggests that in the spirit of competition, were it not for the NOCSEA stamp, we might issue the kids AK-47s or spitting cobras.

During All-Star play, we ran into one umpire who was a self-appointed guardian of the NOCSEA rule. As I sometimes do (I just can't help myself in these situations), I did my best to raise a fuss about it.

"What if we took this same helmet and peeled off that NOCSEA seal?" I asked. "Could we still use that helmet? Would it still be safe for kids even though the seal is gone?"

"Nope," said the ump. "I would have to throw it out of the game."

I wouldn't let go of the conversation. "Maybe you can explain to me how that teensy-weensy piece of paper, which must be about a millioneth of an inch thick, keeps a kid from getting hurt."

He gave me his God-spare-me-from-smart-alecks look, then responded with the cry that has prevailed since the dawn of bureaucracy.

"Look, I don't make the rules. I'm just doing what they tell me."

We advanced to the Division II Tournament, in which perhaps the most competitive Little League baseball in the United States is played. Division II includes about 900 teams in Southern California. The team that wins the tournament often goes on to win the western region and go to Williamsport.

One of our games was a seesaw battle against a fine team called Deer Canyon. By the bottom of the sixth (the last inning in Little League), we were leading 4 to 3. With two outs and two men on, a Deer Canyon batter hit a sharp grounder between third and short. Ryan Beaver, playing third, dove for it. The ball took a bad hop over his glove.

Rushing to deep short, Sean backhanded the ball and threw a rocket to first for the final out. If the ball had hit Ryan's glove, we might have lost. It was the best Little League game I'd ever seen. But I didn't know then there would be an even better game not far down the road.

For all the angst caused by umpires, parents, and the sons of parents, we were having some fun times. And, occasionally, some crazy times. The business with the troll dolls was a good example.

Looking back on the season, I'm not sure when and where the troll doll explosion started. I'm talking about those rubbery-looking, smiling dolls, with the knee-torn denims and wild, fluorescent hair.

They became the team mascot. And they multiplied like kangaroos. Everytime I looked around, troll dolls were looking back from the stands, or from family cars, or from foul screens, in which our team parents would insert them before each game. Soon, they were even showing up in the dugout. Then, later, on televised news reports of Long Beach games.

Our fields of play began to look like that final scene in "Gremlins," in which the little creatures take over the entire town. I did not know entirely who was behind this, but I do suspect that Deborah, my wife, was spending a good deal of my baseball pension on troll dolls.

It came down to our needing one victory to get to the western tournament in San Bernadino. Our opponent was the All-Star team from Northridge, the Los Angeles suburb later devastated in the January 1994 earthquake.

Dane Mayfield was pitching. After our batters gave him a seven-run lead, he started getting a bit wild. I called time and went to the mound.

"Just throw strikes," I said. "Let them hit it."

"Okay."

The next pitch was a perfect strike, and the Northridge shortstop hit it about nine miles over the fence. It landed on the roof of a building beyond right field.

"Hey, Dane," I called over to him. "I didn't mean for you to take me literally. I was just trying to get a point across."

I started laughing. So did Dane. He then settled down and struck out the side to send us to San Bernardino.

I was now more consumed by Little League baseball than I had been by any previous endeavor of my life, including major-league baseball.

But I had a personal problem that illustrates just how consumed I had become.

With the team now heading for San Bernardino, I was scheduled to play in an old-timers game in Denver. In normal times, I would have pounced on an opportunity like that. Since I left major-league baseball before the advent of multi-million-dollar contracts, I welcome the honoraria that come from playing in such games.

For some flattering reason, David Chavez, the guy promoting the game in Denver, really wanted me there. A couple of days before the game he left a message on my answering machine at home, asking if I was to be in Denver the next morning.

Talk about being jerked back into the real world. I had forgotten about my promise to be in Denver. On the other hand, I had told this guy I would go. What was I to do?

You guessed it. I let Larry handle it.

Larry had a heck of a time getting Chavez on the phone. It was late at night, and he called here and there. When he finally got him, he said he was Jeff Burroughs's lawyer, and that he was going to see Jeff in a couple of hours, but meanwhile...

The guy was beside himself. "Oh, this is wonderful. This is fantastic. I'm so glad you'll be seeing Jeff. I was starting to think maybe he wasn't coming. Write this down: Tell him that if he catches the 7 a.m. flight to Denver tomorrow morning, I'll even pay him double. Tell him we've even named a dog after him, a racing dog. No kidding, the dog's name is Jeff Burroughs. Tell Jeff that and have him call me. Are you writing all this down?"

Since Larry was calling on his car phone and driving at something close to the speed of a locomotive, he wasn't writing anything down. He did not understand all that racing dog stuff anyway. (Nor did I.) What Larry was mostly doing was trying to get the guy to shut up long enough to hear him. That finally happened.

"Look, I may be able to get Jeff to call you, although the odds are against that. Meanwhile, I have to tell you that if I were you, I really would not count on Jeff's showing up in Denver tomorrow."

Chavez would not accept reality. "Please, please, have him call me," he kept saying.

When Larry got to San Bernadino, he told me Chavez had scheduled an old-timers practice for 9 a.m. the next morning in Denver, and that he would pay me double to come.

The bottom line, I'm ashamed to say, is that I stiffed the guy. But I did it for the kids. And for Little League. And all the moms and dads, grandmoms and granddads, and so on.

Yes, there were some problems because of that.

I let Larry handle them.

six

DAVID GONZALEZ

Height: 5'1"
Weight: 126

A key member of the team as a pinch hitter. Had a double and scored a run in Long Beach's 4–3 victory over Beaverton, Oregon, in the first game of the Western Regionals. In all-star play, David hit a home run and batted .385. When he wasn't hampered by a sore right arm, he occasionally filled in at third base.

San Bernardino, where 14 All-Star teams compete each year for the western U.S. Little League championship, is only 75 miles from Long Beach. But driving there is like driving from the Temperate Zone into downtown Hell.

When it is 110 degrees in San Bernardino, which, in fact, it is much of the time, it is usually about 75 degrees with a breeze beside the ocean in Long Beach. In August, San Berdoo, as the locals call it, is hot, hot, hot, dry, dry, dry—the kind of place where, at any moment, you expect to encounter giant lizards and/or Indiana Jones.

Some of us drove out in a small caravan from Long Beach. A couple of cars broke down on the way. Oblivious as usual to anything that did not involve the team directly,

Larry and I did not know about the problems of our stricken motorists until long after they were no longer problems.

We were about the last team to check in. The tournaments in other states and in Northern California had finished three or four days earlier, and the winners, consequently, had beaten us to San Berdoo.

Initially, I was upset that they had the jump on us. However, I quickly realized that the less time we spent in San Bernardino, the better off we were.

After our 1991 All-Star team lost and was out of the tournaments, I had gone to San Bernardino to see how good the competition was at that level. Having been there, I now had some idea what to expect from the place. For the rest of our team and parents, however, it was a real shocker.

It was 107 degrees when we arrived around five in the afternoon. We lugged our bags into the compound where the kids live during the tournament. The compound is surrounded by fences, barbed wire, and guards, and, except for an Olympic-size swimming pool, looks more like an internment camp than a facility for Little Leaguers.

Located next to the stadium, the team barracks were cement and steel structures. The Little League hosts called them cabins, although cabins were the last thing they looked like. Two teams shared each building, and were separated by a cement wall. Larry and I walked into our building, which we were sharing with the All-Stars from Montana.

It was sweltering. Each half of a cabin was cooled— make that allegedly cooled—by an air conditioner that really is not an air conditioner, but an ice-and-water affair with a fan. Called a "swamp cooler," these devices had stopped working sometime around Woodstock. If you positioned yourself directly under the vent and there was no one else in the cabin with you, it was possible to feel a faint wisp of cool air.

The place had the trappings of those "boot camps" some states have developed in an effort to make young criminals go straight. Each half cabin had seven bunk beds with two tiers for the players. My first thought was, "We're risking injuries. These kids have never slept in bunk beds before. Someone is certain to fall off one of them."

Sure enough. Nights to come were punctuated by an occasional loud crash at three in the morning. Fortunately, there were no injuries. The kids being as sloppy as they were (and Larry and I being as undisciplinary as we were), the falls were cushioned by piles of clothing and equipment strewn about the floor. For once, the team's slovenly lifestyle paid off.

Larry and I had it better than the kids. But not much better. We had a tiny room with a door we could close to escape them. There were single beds (smaller than the beds the kids had) and a hanging locker for each of us.

I'm six-foot-one and a bit over 200 pounds. The beds, I found, were so small, you couldn't really turn over normally. You had to kind of flip like a fried egg—almost jump up from the bed and come down on your other side. It was really a terrific room—if you knew how to levitate.

We looked around our room, which took two seconds, then looked at each other. "You know what?" Larry said. "If I had known it was going to be this bad, we might have thrown a game or two along the way and gotten eliminated." We laughed.

The Long Beach All-Stars arrived at the compound after Larry and me, and they immediately got busy misbehaving and complaining about the heat. The wall that separated us from the Montana kids was surprisingly effective. We couldn't hear them, although I'm sure Montana kids can be as noisy as any in the West.

The place fit my image of those Chinese rehabilitation camps where people are sent for saying the wrong thing. Small wonder that the parents of players were not allowed inside. Had they seen the place, they might have pulled their kids out and gone home.

There was a mess hall, which you could enter only if you had a pass and were not wearing a hat. (In fact, you needed a pass to get into the compound.) A voice on the loudspeaker would boom out, "California, first call lunch," and our kids would shuffle off to the mess hall like a chain gang from a Paul Muni movie.

To kids who depend on television the way fish depend on water, the most Spartan feature of San Bernardino was the fact that there was only one TV set in the entire compound. It was located in the "information room," and teams supposedly could reserve it to watch videos of the game played the night before.

Next to swimming (we didn't want the kids to do too much of that for fear it would tire their muscles) and a trip to Disneyland or some such outing, there was little else for the kids to do except trade pins.

A separate book probably could be written about pin-trading. It is, I think the favorite pastime in Little League, with baseball running a close second.

Throughout the world, Little League districts that can afford to do so have their own pins made—and are constantly issuing new ones. San Bernardino even had a huge tent set up strictly for pin-traders. It was jammed almost all the time with devotees of all ages.

Some Little Leaguers would much rather trade pins than play baseball. Our older son, Scott, came to San Bernardino the year before strictly to trade pins. Like other Long Beach kids, he started out with a war chest of about 50 pins, given to him by local League officials. His collection, one of the largest in the U.S., now numbers about 10,000.

Larry was especially naive about the regional playoffs. There was a big case coming up at his law firm, and some junior attorneys were working under him in preparation for it. His plan was to manage the team for a game, then drive to the office to do some legal work, then drive back to San Bernardino for the next game.

There was a meeting for managers and coaches that first evening. We went around, and people from the 14 teams introduced themselves.

A coach from the Oregon team got up and said, "My name is Greg Barton." Larry and I almost fell over. He and Barton had been classmates at Miliken High School in Long Beach. I remembered Greg from when he broke a bunch of records as quarterback for Long Beach City College. He had gone on to play for the Detroit Lions and a few other NFL teams.

A really nice guy, he became a great help in telling us what to expect at the western regional tournament. He had been there four or five times with teams from Oregon.

The main purpose of the meeting was to acquaint us with the rules of play for the tournament. Now, I'm not much on rules and regulations. So when they passed around a list containing more than 50 rules, I was ready to fake kidney stones to get out of there.

The amazing thing was that this was not even the entire list of rules for the tournament. They were only the *new* rules, the ones making their debut in 1992. Larry and I took one look at them and got hysterical.

At that moment, a little fellow named Sy took over the meeting. I never did learn Sy's last name, but he was the tournament's chief umpire, a position which, people told me, he had held for about 100 years. After the rules were handed out, Sy gave the same heart-warming welcome address he apparently had been giving for the past century.

"These are the rules. You better get used to them."

At that instant, I decided I hated Sy more than any person I'd ever known.

Surprisingly, we later became pretty good friends. But right then, with the temperature still over 100 degrees and feeling desperate for the meeting to end, I loathed the man.

While playing professional baseball, I got to know umpires off the field. Most are nice people, but still there is something different about people who choose that profession. It's almost as if they were raised for it, the way sheep are raised for wool. Many of them become quite accomplished at being real grouchy at walking the earth as if they know more than the rest of us mere humans.

Sy went on and on. We already had been at the meeting for about an hour and a half. Back in the cabin, there were a million things that needed to be done to get the team ready. Also, the fact that no other adults were allowed into the compound at that point meant that the kids were alone. And probably burning down the place.

But Sy, who loved to talk as much as anyone on the planet, was oblivious to our concerns.

"Get out your rule sheets," he said. "Rule Number One..."

I couldn't believe it. Instead of saying, "Please review the rules before your first game," he planned to read every one of them. I had a premonition that in 12 days, when the tournament was to end, we would still be listening to Sy. Or that in a thousand years, a prospector would find our skeletons—with Sy's bones clutching the sheet of rules.

Sy did not really read. He barked. With all the charm of a guard in a gulag, he went over the rules in a way that said, "Don't even think about questioning them." He made us feel as if every person in the room already was in trouble. You could feel collective hate building for the guy. Managers and coaches were thinking, "If we're as dumb as Sy thinks we are, how did we ever manage to get here?"

A few people were dumb enough to ask questions. When they did, the others would groan and brace themselves for a 20-minute answer from Sy.

The rules (I don't know if they were Little League's rules or Sy's) were amazing. They were designed to cover situations that probably would not take place between now and the next ice age.

My favorite was the sunflower-seed rule. It was illegal for a player to spit a sunflower seed on the field. Why this admonition against sunflower seeds? Why no rule against, say, crack cocaine?

For seven weeks, our kids had worked their little tails off to get to this tournament. They had practiced hard, played hard. They had won tough, nail-biting games. And now someone was saying it could come down to a final game with one of our guys hitting a home run, only to be ejected for spitting a sunflower seed while rounding third base. Who dreams up this garbage? Why don't they just let the kids play baseball?

It was about 9:30 by then—and the beginning of the end for Larry, who had earlier entertained thoughts of fleeing to his office to prepare for that big case. He phoned his partners, and said something like, "Good luck on the case. See you in a couple of weeks."

A bit more needs to be said about umpires. In the western tournament, umpiring is a status thing. As I understand it, there is a waiting list of volunteer umpires. Any adults who have made their marks in Little League are eligible so long as their home leagues certify them as "dedicated volunteers."

Once you submit your name to umpire, years may pass before you are called. Joe Doe sends in his name, five years pass, and he gets a letter inviting him to umpire at that year's tournament. By then, Joe Doe may be out of baseball and may even have had a frontal lobotomy and forgotten the rules. But he rumages through his attic or garage, finds his umpire's cap, and says, "Bye, honey, I'm off to San Bernardino."

In the majors, I got to know great umpires, guys like Doug Harvey. They considered a well-umpired game to be one in which you hardly realized umpires were there. But some Little League umpires—not all—really want to make that big call that will decide the outcome of a game. Somtimes, just making the call matters more to them than whether the call is correct.

As mentioned, I had watched the previous year's western tournament. Al Huntley, the intense Little League manager from Long Beach, had come with me to study the caliber of play. But it was the caliber of umpiring that was most astonishing. We had never seen umpiring like it. The kids were the best in the west, but the umpires were awful.

A close call at the plate is one thing, a matter of human judgement. But in the tournament there was always the risk that a team could rise or fall on a bad decision by an ump who did not have a clue about the rules.

Al and I saw one call that was absolutely amazing. With the bases loaded, a pitcher for the Hawaii team hit a Nevada batter on his kneecap. The ball ricocheted all the way to the third-base dugout. The batter limped toward first.

At this point, the plate umpire, a guy the size of a gnome, should have stepped in front of the plate, called time, and awarded first base to the batter while the runners advanced a base. Instead, he did nothing. It's like the game was in San Bernardino and he was on Neptune.

Nevada's third-base coach saw the ball lying at his feet. With no fielders going after it and no time out called, he started to wave the runners around. Finally, someone on the defensive team grabbed the ball and threw it about two feet over the catcher's head just as two Nevada guys were sliding into home plate almost at the same time.

There was dust and confusion. Coaches were screaming. Parents were screaming. Kids were jumping up and down. Four runs had scored, and still the umpire had done nothing except watch everyone circle the bases.

Hawaii's coach rocketed out of the dugout, which the rules say he is not supposed to do. (You cannot come out of the dugout unless you call time and are cleared by the umpire.) He was screaming, "What's going on? The kid got hit by a pitch. It's supposed to be a dead ball."

This is a rule kids grasp at about the age of seven, but the umpire was totally lost. Everybody in the ballpark knew he had made the wrong call—or, actually, no call. Ultimately, another umpire persuaded him to rectify the situation.

Postscript: A couple of games later, the same guy was working a game as left field umpire when a batted ball landed on the foul line. He called out, "Foul ball," as if he were umpiring a Shakespearean drama.

Another argument ensued, with the offensive team arguing, correctly, that a ball that hits the foul line is a fair ball. But the umpire insisted it was foul. He probably said something like, "That's why they call it the foul line and not the fair line."

Toward the end of the San Bernadino tournament, when I got to know Sy better (and, oddly, decided I liked him), I told him that I thought the caliber of umpiring the previous year had been terrible.

To my surprise, he agreed. "That was one of the worst batches of umpires we ever had here. They came a few days early, but I just could not train them."

For 1992, he had tried to improve the situation. And most of the '92 umpires did a pretty good job. They made a few bad calls. But at least they knew the rules.

Still, there was cause to worry, as evidenced by a conversation I had in the cafeteria with one of the umpires. We had been chatting with several of them, nice guys all, when one suddenly said, "I don't believe in ending a game by calling a child out on a called third strike. No matter where the pitcher throws the ball, I'll never call a kid out in that situation if he does not swing at the ball."

"Interesting," I said. "Why is that?"

"I just don't believe it's fair to the batter. It doesn't matter if the score is tied or whatever. I'll never call the batter out on a called third strike?"

"What about the pitcher?" I asked. "That's not very fair to him."

"That's not the same," he replied. "The hitter gets more stressed out than the pitcher does."

I'm not sure why he told us that, unless he wanted to show how he's a tough guy and really has a handle on the game. But I remembered the conversation after the tournament began—and he wound up as the home-plate umpire for one of our games.

Sore point: The umpires at San Bernardino were housed in the only building at the compound that was truly air-conditioned. And to think some of us had the notion that Little League is supposed to be for the kids.

seven

JEFF WARSHAUER

Height: 5'2"
Weight: 110

Jeff was one of the team's unsung
heroes. On a team of offensive
players, Warshauer, a two-time
all-star, earned his laurels behind
the plate, where he played error-
free ball as starting catcher in all 17
playoff games.

Because of its population, California is allowed two teams
in the western tournament.

In fact, Northern and Southern California are
usually the tournament favorites. With so many leagues
operating in California, kids from that state have had
more competition than other western teams by the time
they get to San Bernardino. (Hawaii, where they play a
lot of year-round baseball, usually fields a good team as
well.)

This year, the favorite was the Northern California
team from San Ramon Valley. That is Contra Costa County, part of the Bay Area. More exactly, the team was from
the Blackhawk area of San Ramon Valley, where some

houses had price tags in the millions of dollars. I had lived in those parts (the low-rent district) while playing for the Oakland A's and was familiar with the area.

San Ramon had gone to Williamsport as the 1991 champs of the western U.S. (They had been beaten in the final game by a team from Taiwan, the country that had been dominating Little League World Series play.)

The San Ramon parents were certain their boys would repeat. They even had made hotel reservations in Williamsport.

Having told you about hating Sy, the chief umpire, I hesitate to make the confession that is about to unfold. You may think I am some sort of social misfit. But, misfit or not, here goes:

I hate San Ramon Valley. More, even, than I hated Sy.

Yes, I know. Adults are not supposed to hate kids. In San Ramon's case, however, it took a lot of work not to hate the kids. There were some exceptions, of course, but most of those dear little tykes reminded me of that movie, "Children of the Corn," in which the kids lived out on a prairie and killed anyone who came near them.

Okay, San Ramon's kids were not quite that bad. But neither were they much better. One of their favorite things was to scream at our kids and make fun of them in the swimming pool. They particularly enjoyed making fun of Sean and would mockingly ask for his autograph. By the time the tournament ended, they had managed to irritate practically everyone in the complex.

Since kids, as noted earlier, pretty much reflect their parents, a volatile chemistry developed between the San Ramon and Long Beach adults. Irrational as my hatred of San Ramon may have been, I was not alone. Larry hated them, too. So did our team parents, our team fans, and our team pets. We're talking heavy-duty antagonism: David and Goliath, Rome and Carthage.

To me, the greatest San Ramon annoyance was the team's manager, a miserable entity named Chickie Walsh, of whom you will read more.

San Ramon's coaches, parents, supporters, and others seemed to have come to Southern California with umpteen tons of video equipment. Their brand of baseball involved taping games, then repairing to hotel rooms to sip wine, play the videos, and try to master the rival coaches' signals. They put a camcorder on me while we were beating another team—and kept it on me through the game. Apparently, they spent hours trying to figure my signals.

To a degree, most Little League teams did that sort of thing, but only San Ramon did it with the intensity given to trying to break the Japanese codes in World War II.

Chickie, their manager, had a big role in this effort, and approached it with the subtlety of the Three Stooges. From the dugout, I called the pitches, signaling them to our catcher, Jeff Warshauer, who relayed them to the pitcher. Chickie watched me as if I were his banker.

Convinced he had cracked our code, he went to work. If he thought I called for a fastball, he would shout the San Ramon batter's first name. If he thought the pitch was going to be a curve, he would shout the batter's last name. (Not that it made any difference. At that stage in their young lives, a curveball is like a UFO to a Little Leaguer. They don't know how to react to it. And, in most cases, they don't have enough reaction time anyway.)

In the long run, Chickie's silly stuff probably helped us because his first-name and last-name codes were simply one more thing San Ramon's batters had to worry about.

In time, Chickie really did master our signals. When he did, however, we had some fun at Chickie's expense. I called time, and told Jeff Warshauer our catcher, "Let's screw these guys up." We changed the signs around. What Chickie thought was a fastball was now a curve, and so on.

Jeff was great. He never missed a signal. For about three innings, we screwed them up—with Chickie all the while shouting out first names and last names. Finally, he figured out what happened, and he gave up trying to alert his guys to the pitches.

Chickie had been quoted in a newspaper story on the difference between players from San Ramon and those from other teams. I no longer have the clipping, but he said something like, "We come from a white-collar area. As adults and parents, we teach our children to be competitive and win—and to win at a very early age. Our kids are not blue-collar kids. They are white-collar kids, and their white-collar parents are more succesful as a whole than blue-collar parents."

What a jerk!

We got a real break in San Bernardino because our games were at night. Other teams played some of their games at 10 a.m. or noon, when the temperature was about 110 degrees, sometimes higher.

There was a reason for our night games. Always with an eye on the cash box, Little League officials scheduled our games at night because, being from only 75 miles away, we were the team most likely to draw the largest crowds. And while there is never an admission charge to a Little League game, they do pass the hat—or, in the case of

San Bernardino, the money canister. And, of course, there was money to be made at the concession stands.

It was a good strategy. As the games went on, we really did start to pull in fans from the Long Beach area. It helped that the Dodgers and Angels, the major-league teams closest to Long Beach, were having awful seasons. Suddenly, fans starved for victory began to discover this Little League team that had yet to lose a game.

Our first opponent was Oregon. Wonderful, wonderful kids. Hardly had the game started when our guys, who had come from behind to win so many times, reverted to their old ways. They got behind by four runs.

But Sean got up in the first inning. Although we had not yet played a game in San Bernardino, he already was getting some press, plus a reputation as a good ballplayer.

Seanie went for a curveball and hit it a billion feet. It landed on the roof of the Snack Shack beyond right field. It would have been a homer in most major league ballparks except for one thing. It was a foul ball. Still, it made people take notice.

Our guys waited until the fifth inning to get serious. With Sean pitching, we won the game, 6 to 4.

The tournament was a double elimination. If you lost a game, you were still in competition. But to stay alive, you had to win every game from then on.

Next, we played Alaska. Another great bunch of kids. The team was from Fairbanks, where I have a lot of relatives, and I got a kick out of meeting people who knew my aunts and uncles.

Alaska is not real big on baseball because the state has such a short summer and because they draw players from a relatively small population. In all the years of playing in the western tournament, I think Alaska has won only one game.

Still, they put a kid on the mound against us who was pretty good. He really put the press on us, until our boys got the home-run bug. Ryan Beaver pitched, and we won, 13 to 2.

Meanwhile, our wonderful friends from San Ramon Valley had drawn a bye in the first round, meaning they did not have to play at all. The teams are drawn out of a hat, and that's just the way things broke. Then they were scheduled to play Idaho, a game they were almost assured of winning. (In the end, San Ramon barely won that game.)

Chickie kept trying to needle us by saying that San Ramon had the toughest schedule while we had the easiest. But Montana and Idaho, both on Chickie's schedule, were two of the easiest teams. Being from states with smaller populations, they have less competition in the battle to get to San Bernardino.

In the cabins, day and night, the temperature almost never dropped below Unbearable. And the kids, rather than being wiped out by the heat, seemed determined to drive Larry and me to the crazy house.

Take sleepwalking, for example. There has not been a whole lot written about the relationship between sleepwalking and baseball, but it was a prime concern for those of us charged with the responsibility of overseeing the Long Beach All-Stars.

Sleepwalking is, of course, common to kids. In our case, however, we had a couple of world-class walkers. Ali was probably the best. He would sit up in the middle of the night, jump off his top bunk, hit the floor like the 101st Airborne, trot around, and never wake up.

Ryan Beaver was pretty good, too. One night, he walked into the coaches' room at about three o'clock. Larry woke up and engaged him in conversation.

"What are you doing?"

"Just walking around."

"Where are you going?"

"I don't know. Nowhere special."

"Maybe you ought to go back to bed."

"Okay."

Beav's mom and dad confirmed that he did that sort of thing all the time at home.

As if we did not have enough trouble trying to discipline the kids, we had another of those God-save-us-from-the-parents episodes. This one involved our concealed-identity figure from Chapter Three—Dad X.

Dad X is fond of lecturing anyone who will listen on the importance of good health and good food, blah-blah-blah. That made it all the more memorable when we caught him smuggling in a supply of Snickers candy bars to his son (with the aforementioned pseudonym, Egbert).

"You really think this is a smart thing to do?" I asked Dad X.

"Egbert said he was hungry."

"Yeah? Well, when he's hungry, why don't you bring him asparagus or something? There's enough sugar in those candy bars to make a small nation go crazy. Don't bring him this stuff. It gets the kids worked up. Then you leave, and Larry and I are stuck with the little animals for hours."

Larry got real concerned at one point because the kids appeared to be reverting to baby talk. When he got really worked up about things, Larry himself reverted to talking like a lawyer. In this case, he said something like "I am aghast that they would engage in this method of communication."

He was really in a stew and ready to phone whatever is the psychiatric counterpart of 9-1-1.

I put him at ease. "That isn't baby talk, Larry. It's Bart Simpson talk. They're talking like a character on the Simpsons TV program."

It appears I watch more television than Larry.

This is probably as good a place as any to hand out the awards for disruptive behavior in the barracks. The hands-down winners were Randall Shelley, Ali Strain-Bay, and, flesh of my flesh, Sean. They were the ringleaders.

Randall, a nice but mischievous kid and a neighbor of ours, was not pleased at being lumped together with the other nefarious cohorts. He confronted Larry one day, and said, "I heard that Jeff told my mom I was one of the worst kids on the team. Is that really true?"

Larry said, "Well, I don't know that you're the absolute worst, but congratulations, you have been nominated."

Ali was the champ of sneakiness. (Maybe it had something to do with his sleepwalking.) He will make a great commando someday. From the coaches' room, we would hear a bout of giggling, followed by the patter of Little League feet. One of us would go out to the big room and turn on the light just in time to spot Ali diving back into bed.

Ali was also the orchestra leader. Around 4 a.m. or there-abouts, he would bounce ever so slightly on his bunk bed.

S-c-r-e-e-c-h.

Someone else would join in by bouncing on his bed.

S-c-r-e-e-c-h. S-c-r-e-e-c-h.

Soon, they were all doing it, and the total effect was like listening to the Los Angeles Philharmonic playing off-key.

Larry and I would rush from our room to catch the villain (knowing full well it was probably Ali). But trying to get him in the act was like trying to catch a mouse. But by the time we turned on the light, they were all feigning sleep.

We would go back to our room, get in bed, and start to drift off to sleep.

S-c-r-e-e-c-h. S-c-r-e-e-c-h. S-c-r-e-e-c-h.

Individually, these guys are the best-behaved kids you could ever imagine. But the pack mentality did something to them. Together, they were horrendous.

Eventually, it reached a point where Larry and I had spent so much time with the little guys that we were ready for the asylum. We were getting about two hours of sleep a night. It was too hot, too noisy, too everything. The kids were misbehaving terribly and we, as noted, were terrible disciplinarians. The kids found us about as intimidating as Tinkerbell.

But we had a secret weapon. John Beaver.

In addition to being a businessman (and team statistician), Ryan's dad is an ordained minister who has specialized in youth work. He is also one tough cookie and does not believe in coddling. When his own kids were six or seven, they would play tackle football and he would run right over them. Full speed. When the kids complained, he would pick them up by the shirt and fling them back to the line of scrimmage.

So, John became our secret weapon. On nights before games, to enable Larry and me to slip away to the Hilton and get some sleep, we brought in John (after getting clearance from tournament officials).

He was exactly what we needed. A screamer. I would give anything to be like him.

He required that lights be out by 10 p.m., and he had a routine that began 15 minutes earlier. He would throw a mattress in the middle of the floor. That was where he planned to sleep. Then, he would walk around and give each kid a piece of licorice. At 10 o'clock, to the second, lights would go out and John would tell the kids to shut up. If there was even a slight peep, John would scream the offender into petrified silence.

The kids obeyed John quite a bit, certainly more than they obeyed Larry and me. He spent every night before a game in the barracks, and he may have been the one adult who did more than Larry and I to get the kids to the top of Little League baseball.

Now and then, with permission, we were able to get the kids out of the compound. They liked the Hilton, its food, and its air-conditioning—not necessarily in that order.

David Gonzalez was kicking back in Denny's room one day. Denny was out somewhere. No sooner did he get back when there was a knock on his door. Standing there was a guy from room serivce, balancing about $40 worth of food on a tray.

"What's this?" asked Denny.

"Your order."

Denny looked around. David was sitting there with a nervous smile.

During one respite at the Hilton, Randall Shelley sat down at the hotel's piano and began to play. An employee stopped him, claiming that the lad was likely to damage the instrument.

At the time, Randall was playing a piece by Chopin.

We were scheduled to play the Hawaii team next. Considering all the time I had spent in the majors, I never would have dreamed this would turn out to be the most exciting baseball game of my life.

eight

DANE MAYFIELD

Height: 5'7"
Weight: 110

This two-time all-star was an exceptional pitcher (5–0) and leadoff hitter. Unfortunately, a sore left elbow kept him from the last two games of the Western Regionals and from pitching in the World Series. Dane hit an amazing .422 over 14 games.

Rumors travel through Little League with the speed of light. Back in the sectional tournament, there was an incredible rumor going around that one team had a pitcher who threw the ball with the speed of light and was about the size of a woolly mammoth. As is the case with most rumors, this one turned out not to be true.

But almost from the start at San Bernardino, another rumor was going around that Hawaii had a pitcher who was beyond belief. And this rumor was true.

He had a somewhat lilting name, Lanakila Niles, and he was a good six feet tall, which is saying something for a 12-year-old. He had a good curveball and was clocked at 82 miles an hour—faster than anyone I had seen in Little League. The word was around that he had never given up a hit. Not one. If there is anyone from 1992 Little League who will make a baseball mark in the future, it is apt to be Lanakila Niles.

Our brain trust got together and wondered how we were going to beat this guy. To work our practice session, we resorted to the combination that had gotten us through batting practice throughout the All-Star season. Chad Stuart, Ryan's older brother, had pitched in college and was still a young man. Al Huntley, although an old geezer like me, could throw the ball forever. And yours truly still had a passable throwing arm.

There were several practice fields at the San Bernardino complex, and you got one by signing up for it. The gangsters from San Ramon Valley were great at figuring at ways to get around everything, and they got around the sign-up procedure simply by signing up for every field. This enabled them to get the best field time after time. How they got away with doing that I don't know, but I do know I was disliking them more with each passing minute.

Well, the brain trust came up with a pretty good idea. We loaded the kids into our cars and drove into the town of San Bernardino, where we had found a field on which to practice. As fields go, it was sort of a dust bowl. There was virtually no grass. When the sun hit it, the reflection backed up into your face and you might as well have been standing in the Sahara.

Steve Warshauer, the grand-old-man member of the brain trust at age 50, caught for the practice with full catching gear on. In fact, he had caught for all our practices. I don't know how he did it.

As we always did in practice sessions, we decided to play a practice game. But this time there would be a difference. We would throw to the kids as hard as we could.

If Dad X thought we had thrown tough to Egbert in that one practice sesssion, he would have had a stroke had he seen this one. I mean, we had always thrown hard to the kids, but this time we put our lives on the line. Well, at least our pitching arms.

We went through the batting order a couple of times, and the kids had a bit of a rough time. Then they started getting used to the pitches. Soon, they were hitting these bullets. Passers-by stopped to watch and were pretty impressed. So was I. By the time the session ended, the kids were hitting everything.

Personally, I found it pretty embarrassing to find I could not throw the ball past an 11- or 12-year-old. That's how good they had become. Or how bad my arm had become.

We were as ready as we could ever be for Lanakila Niles and the Hawaii team. Thus began one of the greatest Little League games in the history of mankind.

The game started on a slightly ominous note. Remember that umpire who had told me he would never end a game by calling a kid out on the third strike? There he was. Behind the plate. "Please, God," I thought, "don't let the outcome of this game wind up in this guy's hands."

We put Dane Mayfield on the mound. During the regular season, he had been having trouble with his shoulder. We were concerned about it and were not willing to settle for taking him just to a local doctor. So we took him up to the Jobe-Kerlan Clinic, one of the finest sports medical facilities in the United States, and got Lewis Yocum, the team physician for the California Angels. Dr. Yocum decided it was probably tendonitis.

There was nothing mysterious about tendonitis. He suggested Dane not pitch for four or five weeks, then start throwing again. If it still hurt, stop throwing. Simple as that.

When Dane did start throwing again, he came around and won six or seven games for the All-Stars. There was no reason not to throw him against Hawaii. Or so we thought.

Niles struck out our first two batters on six or seven pitches. Then Sean came up and tagged a slider into left center for a double—perhaps the first hit ever off Niles. (Sean would wind up going 21 for 23, and he would be voted Most Valuable Player in the western tournament.)

The Hawaii pitcher had an expression on his face that said, "Wow! I threw the ball and someone actually hit it!" It shook him a bit. He threw his glove down and began crying a little. But he regrouped very quickly, striking our next batter out. I thought, "How will we ever be able to score a run against this guy?"

Meanwhile, Dane had started off well, laying down the Hawaii batters like clockwork. Even more importantly, he got up in the third and hit one of Niles's super fastballs to right field for a home run. It was one of those right-on-the-line right field homers that had become a trademark of our guys. Score: Southern California 1, Hawaii 0.

Dane continued to pitch well. Alex DeFazio made his usual share of impossible plays. Hawaii stayed right with us. It was a tremendously well-played ball game on both sides. Until the fourth inning.

Hawaii's first batter got a base hit up the middle. Hawaii was not much of a hitting team, but they had good defense and good pitching. They could bunt, however, and they tried bunting on us. We took the bunt away from them by moving our first and third basemen in real close. So far, so good.

But then Dane hung a curveball on their big, left-handed first baseman, Ryan Katsumoto, who parked it over the fence.

I went out to talk to Dane, and he said, "Jeff, my arm is killing me." There was no doubt that it was. The kid was crying.

"Okay," I said. "Come on out."

I may be leaving myself open for criticism by having pitched a kid when his arm was bad. But we had medical clearance to pitch Dane. And he had not had any trouble for three months or more. Moreover, the problem this time was not his shoulder, it was his elbow. The next day, it had swelled to the size of a grapefruit.

Now and then, someone will say the curveball should be outlawed in Little League. Maybe they have a point. I think managers sometimes let kids throw the curve before the kids are really ready to do it. I followed a policy of letting a kid throw the curve only if he showed the proper form for throwing it. Further, I had them throw more of a slow-change curve than the snapping, twisting motion commonly associated with the curve.

Dane had tremendous form. He had been throwing the curve well for some time. But I suspect he was growing so fast that his bones had not caught up to his muscle structure. It was a problem I had had as a kid playing ball. When I pitched and threw the curve, my tendon would get sore and I would get terrible swelling.

Lest you worry about these Little League pitchers, let me add this: Up to that point, Dane Mayfield was the only Little Leaguer I ever coached who had a sore arm.

Denny Mayfield was crushed. Dane's injury was not career-threatening, but it did mean he would have a limited role if our team survived beyond the San Bernardino tournament. Luckily Dane took it pretty much in stride. He is a very happy camper.

After pulling Dane off the mound, we put Randall Shelley in for the fourth and fifth innings.

In our fifth inning at bat, Niles blew us away, 1-2-3. But Randall pitched exceedingly well when you consider he had not pitched at all in the tournament, and suddenly we put him in there in front of a huge crowd of about 10,000.

When he came off the mound at the end of the fifth, I said, "You did a great job. Next inning, we'll put Sean on the mound to finish up. You've hardly pitched all year. I don't want to put you in a spot where you could get nervous. I don't think it would be fair to you."

Another kid might have protested or cried or something. But Randall, a kid with about a billion freckles, simply said, "Okay, coach." God, I loved those kids.

Having been designated the visiting team, we were first to bat in the sixth and were still trailing, 2-1. I began thinking the game was down the drain. I could not impart that to the kids, of course. Part of my job is to keep them pumped up. It was okay for me to be nervous, but I couldn't let the kids be nervous.

Our first batter struck out. The second was thrown out on a ground ball. Ryan Beaver came to the plate. Niles, clearly the best Little League pitcher in the world, already had struck out 12 guys, and needed only one more out. And he got two strikes on Beav.

Time was called. Larry came out of the dugout, and told Ryan, "As long as we have one strike left, we still have a chance."

To this day, I cannot figure why the Hawaii coach did not have Niles throw a curve or slider into the dirt. With a pitcher who threw that hard, Little Leaguers would swing at any ball thrown into the dirt in that situation. They can't help themselves.

But, wonder of wonders, Niles threw a fastball down the strike zone. Beav tagged it to center field. The wind was blowing a bit. From where I stood at third, I think I was pursing my lips and blowing at the ball to help it along. You could see it was going to be close. The center fielder was back pedaling and the ball was still going back, back. The fielder reached up to catch it.

There was a tiny instant, sort of frozen in time, when you could see the ball was going to land in the kid's glove or soar over it by a fraction of an inch. And at that very instant, the fielder's back hit the fence. It kind of jarred him. He crumpled a bit, and the ball went over his glove and over the fence.

Home run. The game was tied.

Time was called. The Hawaii kid had hurt his back a bit, and there was about a five-minute delay until it was determined he was okay. He stayed in the game.

With two outs and the game tied, Sean came up. In the stands, fans were chanting, "Long Beach! Long Beach!"

Being his father's son, Sean is a bit of a ham. Young as he is, he has a keen sense of what stirs up the media. Somewhere during the season, for example, he started this gimmick about pounding the plate with his bat in order to "summon up the Home Run God." The writers loved it.

Once again, Sean pounded the plate. And, once again, Niles reared back and threw. My boy put it over the left field fence. We were leading, 3 to 2. Niles had given up two homers on two pitches.

Everyone was in shock. In the coach's box, I went down on my knees. In the stands, people were going absolutely nuts as Sean rounded the bases with his 14th home run in All-Star play.

Still, the game was not over. Hawaii was coming to bat. Sean went to the mound. Because he had been in the on-deck circle, then at bat, there had been no time for him to warm up.

He got two men out, one on Jeff Warshauer's great catch of a foul ball. But then Sean gave up a walk, and the next batter got a single. They had men on first and second.

And remember: Behind the plate was that umpire who had said he would never end a game by calling a batter out on a called third strike.

Sure enough, the count went to two balls and two strikes. One more strike and we would win the game and play for the western championship. Sean reared back and threw in right down the middle. Jeff Warshauer was so certain it was a strike that he started toward the dugout. Sean took a step or two off the mound.

"Ball three!" called the umpire. I thought, "It happened! He actually did it! Why in heaven's name would he do something like that?"

On the next pitch, the batter singled up the middle. Randall Shelley charged the ball, grabbed it cleanly, and made a beautiful throw to hold the lead runner at third. But Hawaii had loaded the bases.

Again, Sean got two strikes on the next batter. Again, he threw the next pitch down the middle. And again, incredibly, the umpire called a ball.

Fans were getting on the ump now. "What is this guy doing?" I thought. "Sean could not have thrown a more perfect strike."

My worst nightmare about umpiring seemed about to come true. Hawaii's hitters did not swing at many pitches to begin with, so I figured this kid would never swing and that he would be walked. On the mound, Sean was on the verge of crying from frustration.

With the count two and two, Sean threw again. It would have been a ball. To my amazement, the Hawaii batter swung at it. And missed.

The greatest baseball game of my life was over.

We never said a word to the umpire. There was no point in doing so. On top of that, we couldn't help but feel sorry for the Hawaii kids. After all, this wasn't the World Series, where you want to beat another 30-year-old who plays for the Toronto Blue Jays or Atlanta Braves or whoever.

These were 11- and 12-year-old kids, and you have to feel sorry for any kid who is that heartbroken. Niles was crying so badly after the game, they almost had to carry him to the compound.

Hawaii had turned in a remarkable performance. I went over to congratulate their manager and coach. The fact that they were such genuinely nice people made me feel even worse for them.

Our come-from-behind win had been so phenomenal that some of us even got a bit mystical about it. During All-Star play, the kids had been wearing "R.G." on their uniforms in memory of Ruben Gutierrez, the umpire killed in the hit-and-run accident.

The stadium was ringed by state flags representing the western states competing in the tournament. At the height of tension during the game, while a fairly stiff breeze was ruffling the flags, one of our team moms claimed the California flag was not moving at all. She decided this was a "Go, team" message from Ruben. I was feeling too euphoric myself to question anything like that.

It was Sunday night. The following day, San Ramon defeated Utah—barely. They won by a score of 9 to 8, and they had to come from behind to do it.

Now, of the 14 teams in the tournament, only two were still undefeated—San Ramon Valley and Long Beach.

We would play them Tuesday night.

nine

ALEX DeFAZIO

Height: 4'7"
Weight: 75

The smallest member of the team
was also one of its toughest
defensive players. Alex made key
defensive plays in the Division II
championship game and in the
Western Regionals. He batted ninth
in the order and hit .250, including
three doubles. He scored 12 times...
and broke hearts all along the way.

We were not alone in our unabashed loathing of San
Ramon Valley. The other coaches hated them, too.

Okay, maybe hate is too strong a word here. I'm not
a hateful guy. And who can really hate kids—especially
kids who are playing their hearts out?

On the other hand, San Ramon's adults sure made
me grind my molars.

San Ramon was trying to become the first Little
League team to win back-to-back western championships.
But I don't think they were quite as good as they had been
in 1991.

The previous year's team had been coached by a
good friend and former teammate of mine from my days

with the Oakland A's, Wayne Gross. He had played third base for the A's. I was astonished when, in 1991, I went down to San Bernardino to watch the tournament and saw Wayne's big ugly mug coaching at third base.

Wayne had also played for Baltimore, and he was the most incredible left-handed pull hitter I'd ever seen. Pitchers would throw him balls on the inside of the plate and he would pull them so much, he'd actually hit them over the on-deck circle. I'd never seen anyone do that continuously before or since.

Unfortunately, Wayne was not coaching this year. Had he been with the team, maybe the unpleasantness that existed between our respective camps would have been lessened.

Still, all that mutual dislike did not spring up overnight. In 1991, the Northerners heard their Southern California counterparts had a good bunch of 10-year-old players. They issued an invitation (read challenge) to the 13 leagues of District 38, our district, to take part in a tournament for 10-year-olds, a tournament they would host.

We accepted. Three or four teams from our district—10-year-olds all—went up there and squared off against three or four teams from their district. Let me note that they had good teams. San Ramon, to its credit, is very competitive at every level of Little League.

The kids from our league included the Miller twins, Alex DeFazio and Sean. Before our guys went north, Al Huntley coached them. It paid off. On San Ramon's field, with their umpires, and a home crowd, our kids clobbered them. The first game was 14-2 and the final game, the championship, was 10-2.

Later, they challenged us to a tournament for nine-year-olds. We accepted, but nothing came of it. They left me with the impression they never wanted to face our guys ever again.

Back then, I think, is when the animosity began.

So now we were going up against San Ramon again, this time to determine the Little League champions of the western United States.

They had a third baseman who was pretty good and hit third in their batting order. I was concerned about him, but Sean told me he had pitched against him in the 10-year-olds tournament and had struck him out each time. Role reversal. The player calming down the coach. The son reassuring the father. But it worked. I began to think that maybe San Ramon was not quite as good as I had anticipated.

As might be expected with San Ramon, there were a lot of off-the-field shenanigans. I never decided if Chickie Walsh, their manager, was smart and cagey or if he had been born with irritating genes. But everyone around the compound was starting to dislike the guy.

He complained repeatedly that our kids occasionally left the compound to spend time with their parents. All teams did this, but technically, it was a violation of the rules. Kids of 11 and 12 get lonely for their parents. So, we would shuffle our kids off to the San Bernardino Hilton, which had become central headquarters for Long Beach parents and supporters. The kids could get refreshed via the air conditioning and bask in the glory of being doted on by their parents.

Chickie actually filed a formal complaint against us for doing this. It did not seem to matter to him that his team was doing the same thing. (The hotel also had become San Ramon's central headquarters.)

For all his rat-finking on us, I don't think Chickie himself spent a night in the players' compound the whole time we were there. Any time I walked into the bar of the Hilton hotel, I would find Chickie had gotten there before me.

Earlier, I mentoned the video room in which we could watch tapes of games we had played. On one occasion, Chickie reserved it for four consecutive hours. When his kids finished watching their game on tape, he had them watch it again. Then again. Coaches from other teams wanted to use the room, but they did not have the nerve to ask Chickie and his kids to leave.

If Chickie had been born a laboratory rat, he wouldn't have let the other rats use the maze.

After we beat Hawaii, I ran into Chickie. Instead of saying the perfunctory "Nice game," he said, "Hey, Jeff. We had the gun on that Hawaii pitcher, and do you know what? During the last inning, his fastball fell off by 10 miles an hour. Also, I think he had a better slider than a fastball. I didn't think he threw very hard at all."

I just kept on walking.

Chickie puzzled me. I couldn't decide if he was an idiot or an absolutely brilliant guy who was messing with my head. But as much as he was getting under my skin, I was determined not to let him see I was irritated. It would have given him too much pleasure.

One evening, I dropped into the Hilton bar and was invited to join a group of San Ramon parents. Being from Northern California, they were sipping white wine. I've been around baseball a long time, and I've seen a lot of drinking from Bud to bourbon, but this was the first time I had encountered white wine in close proximity to the game.

The wine-sippers were dolled up to the max. They presented a somewhat staggering array of diamond rings, face lifts, tummy tucks, and their wives had them too!

But they were being surprisingly friendly. We were talking baseball, a subject on which I believe I have some credibility in view of my background. But then along came Chickie. Whenever I ventured an opinion, he would counter with, "No, no, it can't be done like that" or "Let me tell you how we do it."

Let's see. I could kill Chickie right there. Larry could get me out on bail, and there would still be enough time to get to Williamsport.

Perhaps pumped up by Chickie, the parents were saying, "We'll be the first U.S. team to go to Williamsport two years in a row." (Actually, they would not have been the first.)

It took a lot of gall, I thought, to talk about their going to Williamsport when: 1, they still had to beat the Long Beach team, and 2, the manager and coach of the Long Beach team were sitting right there.

They lamented about the tough schedule they'd had in the tournament up to that point. That was ridiculous. Even the people working the concession stands knew that Idaho and Montana, the two teams San Ramon had beaten by then, were pushovers.

They would tell me Sean was "a good little player," but that he does not throw nearly as hard as Lanakila Niles or their own top pitcher, Chris Buchanan. On and on it went. Glasses clinked. They toasted the team's impending success—in Williamsport.

Chickie jumped in once again. "I'll guarantee you one thing. We have a lot better team than you guys. We hit better and there is nobody who can hit off Chris Buchanan (their top pitcher). Nobody's hit him yet, and I don't foresee you guys scoring any runs, whereas I can see our team scoring runs off your pitchers."

I told him he was entitled to his opinion, however stupid it may have been, and let it go at that. But Chickie went on. "I'll guarantee you something else. No 11-year-old pitcher (meaning Sean) will ever beat our vastly superior ballplayers."

I was severely injured that evening. Biting my lips.

It was amusing to wonder what those parents would have thought had they known we had a spy in San Ramon. Really. We had a confederate up there who got copies of their local newspaper to us. It was a small newspaper, but they were covering the San Ramon team the way the *Los Angeles Times* covers the Dodgers. After San Ramon won their first tournament, the team was on the front page for the duration.

The newspapers were invaluable in giving us a better reading of San Ramon's team. And it was a delight to know that, as the saying goes, someone up there liked us.

Don't let me give you the wrong impression. San Ramon did have some neat people (in addition to the spy). For example, Phil Buchanan, the coach who succeeded Wayne Gross, was a terrific person. So was his son, Chris. Next to Niles, Chris was the tournament's best pitcher.

Like Niles, Chris Buchanan had a goatee, a rather unusual accoutrement for a 12-year-old. Because it made him look older than 12, his dad carried the kid's birth certificate in his back pocket. Any time someone would say, "There's no way that kid is 12," Phil Buchanan would produce the certificate and even have it passed around in the stands.

In San Bernardino that year, more people knew when Chris Buchanan was born than knew Abe Lincoln's birthday.

After the drama of the Hawaii contest, Tuesday night's game against San Ramon, much as we had anticipated it, was anticlimactic. Ryan Beaver pitched. "Keep the ball down," I told him. "I don't think these guys can hit very well except for Buchanan." On my advice and plenty of rest imposed by his disciplinarian father the night before, Ryan went the distance.

It was a close game for a while, then our kids exploded. Until that game, Chris Buchanan had not yielded a home run in 86 innings. We got five and won the game, 13-4.

As we were walking off the field, Chickie came up and said, "Chris hurt his thumb sliding the other day and just didn't have his stuff." (There was a rumor that San Ramon had hired a jet to fly Chris to a specialist in Northern California.)

The guy just could not bring himself to give our team any credit. I just shook his hand and walked by him. By now, I really hated him. To me, he just did not feel like a Little League guy.

It was a double elimination tournament, and with the other teams now out, we were to play San Ramon again on Thursday night. If we won, we would be western champs. If they won, we would play them yet again on Friday.

After the first game against San Ramon, our spy sent the newspapers down from Northern California. It was interesting reading. The San Ramon people were quoted as saying that our victory over their team had been a fluke, an aberration that could not possibly happen again. There was no way we could beat them with an 11-year-old pitcher. They, of course, meant Sean. We were going to start him for what we hoped would be the final game.

Our kids were starting to smell Pennsylvania. To give them a break, we got them excused from the compound. They went to a mall in San Bernardino where Alex, true to form, began hitting on a girl working at the Orange Julius counter. She must have been six years older than he was, but he kept at it for a few hours.

His killer line was, "I'm going to Williamsport, babe."

On Wednesday night, Tom Hennessy, a columnist for the *Long Beach Press-Telegram*, received a call at home from an editor. Hennessy has an on-and-off interest in sports. At the moment, it was off.

"If the team wins tomorrow night, we want you to go to Williamsport," said the editor.

"What team?" asked Hennessy.

David Gonzalez, for reasons that probably could not be explained by the Meninger Clinic, suddenly developed a very protective streak toward the team mothers. This consisted mostly of reporting any team father he caught looking at another woman.

At one point, he called over to Sandi Lewis with an alarming bulletin. "Sandi, Sandi, you better get over here right away. Larry's looking at a woman with big breasts."

A fine thing happened before we left San Bernardino. Greg Barton, the Oregon coach who had gone to high school with Larry, asked our lawyer-manager if he would give a little talk to the Oregon players.

Larry did. He told them they should be proud to have gotten as far as they did, and he said that if it had not been for a couple of good breaks we'd gotten, they might be in our place. He talked to them for about 10 minutes. If it had been in their power, I think they would have made him governor of Oregon.

We were making a lot of friends, thanks in part to Chickie Walsh and some of his San Ramon cohorts. Their antics had irritated too many people. A stream of folks from Nevada, Oregon, Alaska, and so on, came by to wish us luck and say things like, "Beat those jerks for us." Even the cafeteria workers had come to dislike San Ramon.

In retrospect, I might have done myself some good by staying away from the Hilton. Among other things, that's where I was when I overheard San Ramon parents discussing the plan. Maybe they were just trying to freak me out. But the plan, real or not, was that Sean would be hit by a pitch during his first at-bat.

Hit hard enough to put him out of the game.

Thursday night's crowd was the largest of the tournament. Al Houghton Stadium seats about 10,000, but there must have been 13,000 people there that night. The excess crowd spilled out onto the grass behind the outfield fence.

Whereas we once only dared to whisper about Williamsport, the newspapers, especially the *Long Beach Press-Telegram*, were running stories about the fact that we only had to win one more game on Thursday to get there. This really built up the Thursday crowd. Several thousand Long Beachers apparently left work early to get on the road before the rush hour.

Before the game, I told the home-plate umpire, whom everybody called Cool Willie, about the possible plan to hit Sean with the ball. I was livid.

"If this happens," I said, "I want Chickie Walsh thrown out of the game. You'll have to throw me out of the game with him because you won't be able to separate my foot from his rear end."

Again, we were the visiting team. As the game began, I was a nervous wreck. With a day off since the last game, San Ramon was able to put Chris Buchanan on the mound again.

Sean led off. Sure enough, the first pitch was right at his head.

He had to hit the dirt to get out of the way. Almost immediately, before I had a chance to call time and remind Cool Willie of our conversation, Buchanan threw a second, and harmless, pitch.

(Cool Willie told me later that not throwing Walsh out of the game then and there was the worst decision he'd ever made as an umpire.)

Buchanan threw again. Sean hit it over the center field fence.

To get a better a look at the team he knew nothing about, Tom Hennessy, the columnist, drove to San Bernardino, grumbling every mile to his wife, Debbie, about his impending assignment in Williamsport: "Why in the world would anyone want to go clear across the United States to watch someone else's kids play Little League baseball?"

By the end of the third inning against San Ramon, he was as rabid a fan as the Long Beach All-Stars would have over the next two years.

Buchanan settled down. He got sharper on the mound and also hit a home run. It was a tight game—until the fifth inning. I think Kevin Miller really got it going. He came up with one out and two men on. I called time and told him, "All I want you to do is hit a ball to the outfield so we can score the guy on third."

I love it when the kids follow my instructions to the letter. On the first or second pitch, Kevin hit a three-run homer to center field. (There were four-baggers, too, by Randall Shelley and Ryan Beaver.)

As Kevin rounded third, I congratulated him. He responded, of course, with an expletive.

That homer really made his season, too. Kevin did not get to play very much in Williamsport later, but for an 11-year-old, he wound up having quite a year.

With the score 11-3 in our favor, San Ramon came up in the sixth. Sean got the first two batters out, and we seemed to have the game in the bag. Then a strange thing happened. Sean walked the next batter. What made that strange was that a lot of people later said Sean had done that on purpose. With that competitive streak of his, the story was that he wanted to end the game by striking out Chris Buchanan.

And he did precisely that, ending the game with a high fastball. To this day, so help me, I have never asked

Sean if he walked that guy on purpose. If I thought for a minute that he had, I might have traded him.

Sean did a little victory dance, and suddenly we were all crying and hugging. The first guy to come over and shake our hands was Chris Buchanan. He is a very classy kid.

Chickie Walsh did shake my hand. "Congratulations," he said. That was it. He just never came around. Instead of admitting defeat, he was like one of those Japanese soldiers who did not come out of the hills to surrender until World War II had been over for 45 years. The nicest thing he said about us was when he later told a reporter that we were "the most patient hitting team" he'd ever seen. That was as close as Chickie came to a compliment.

But right then, I could not have cared less about Chickie Walsh. In the stands, the Long Beach fans were rocking. And by now, just about everyone in the stadium was a Long Beach fan. They cheered wildly as our kids ran the traditional lap around the field while holding aloft the western regional championship banner.

We were the best Little League team in the western United States. And we were going to the Little League World Series in Williamsport, Pennsylvania.

Yahoo!

ten

RYAN BEAVER

Height: 5'7"
Weight: 115

One of Long Beach's explosive hitters, Ryan hit five home runs in the Western Regionals and a total of eight in all-star play. Equally impressive on the mound, this two-time all-star had a 4–0 record and was a major contributor to the team's 1.30 ERA. He also played shortstop and third base.

We wanted to celebrate, but Little League had a different agenda.

After the final San Bernardino game, they whisked our team off the field and took us to a meeting. Carl McGee, Little League's western director, explained a whole new set of rules. (Little League has an endless supply.) We were told who could fly to Pennsylvania at League expense and who could not, and so on.

We got one day off before our Saturday morning flight. Most of the kids went home with their parents to Long Beach. Some families had business to take care of before departing for Williamsport.

Parents are required to dig into their own pockets and pay their own way to Williamsport. So are League presidents and district administrators, the people whose thousands of volunteer hours make Little League successful.

It bugged me that they did not pay the air transportation for the parents, at least. And it bugged me even more when we got to Williamsport and its newspaper, the *Sun-Gazette*, reported that Little League Baseball, Inc., had nearly $20 million in the bank.

Rather than go home, Sean and I stayed in San Bernardino Friday. We were now getting a fair amount of attention from the media in Los Angeles and Long Beach, and if we went home, we'd be leaving ourselves open for that.

So we stayed in the barracks, to which, after 12 days, we had become accustomed—sort of the way convicts become accustomed to Death Row. Ryan Beaver stayed, too. We went to the mall, saw a couple of movies, and kicked back. Meanwhile, my wife, Deborah, had gone home to pay some bills and see if we had any money left.

Not wanting to jinx the team, none of the parents had made any plans to attend the Little League World Series. Now they were doing a lot of scrambling for airline tickets and motel rooms. The latter became a tad easier when the San Ramon parents had to cancel the Williamsport rooms they had reserved.

But that still did not give us enough rooms. Some parents really had a tough time finding places to stay in Williamsport. And, again, I found myself getting peeved at Little League headquarters in Williamsport.

Eight teams, with 14 players each, compete each year at the Little League World Series. That means as many as 112 sets of parents, plus grandparents, other relatives, and friends. It does not take a rocket scientist to figure out that, year after year, a couple hundred hotel rooms will be needed. The moguls of Little League could arrange this with a snap of the finger. But no. Year after year, the parents are left to scramble for themselves.

This was the first in what would become a series of revelations about how Little League Baseball, Inc., functions—or malfunctions—in Williamsport. We were in for a lot of surprises. Behind the scenes, the Little League World Series would prove to be a far different event than the Disney-ish, happy-go-lucky caper projected each year on our television sets.

On Saturday morning, the team flew out of Ontario, a desert airport 100 miles southwest of L.A. Most parents were to fly out the next day from Los Angeles.

The kids had gone home, gotten their uniforms washed and quickly packed. Since they were not professional travelers, they had an excess of luggage, some of it sloppily packed. Combined with the game equipment strewn around the Ontario airport, we looked like a 1990s version of Bingo Long and his Traveling All-Stars.

On the plane, I took inventory. We were on our way to the Little League World Series with:

A kid who could imitate a chicken.
A kid with premature hair on his arms.
A kid with the vocabulary of a rattlesnake.
A kid ready to rat-fink on Larry and me if we glanced at a
    woman.

A kid who communicated with an obscure deity called the
  Home Run God.
A couple of gold-medal sleepwalkers.
Assorted other characters and Bart-Simpson-talkers.
And the world's shortest Don Juan.
What more could a coach want?

After changing planes in St. Louis, we landed in Harrisburg, Pennsylvania, where we were met by our "uncles."
Each of the eight teams competing in Williamsport is assigned a pair of "uncles"—local residents who, in theory, are
supposed to make your stay as comfortable as possible.
Our uncles were a father and son combination. By the time
we left Williamsport, I was ready to feed them to crocodiles.

Along the Susquehanna River, the scenery from
Harrisburg to Williamsport is absolutely gorgeous. Or so I
am told. Since it was pitch black, we could not see a thing.
By the time we pulled into Williamsport, the clock read
1:45. Total travel time from California: 15 hours. By then,
Larry, Denny, and I were numb.

Meanwhile, after being perfectly rotten across the
entire continental United States, the kids, as noted in
chapter 1, managed to fall asleep for the first time about
20 miles outside Williamsport. They were like babies who
cry through the car ride, then fall asleep as you're pulling
into the driveway.

We staggered out of the bus, and there it was—the
dream of every Little Leaguer in the world, or at least of
every Little Leaguer in the world who is paying attention:

Howard J. Lamade Stadium.

Tired as we were and dark as it was, looking at the
home of the Little League World Series was still an enormous thrill. It is a beautiful stadium, with a warning track
and grass that is absolutely gorgeous.

Everyone was starving. We got our gear off the bus while our uncles went to an all-night store and brought back chicken and soft drinks. The kids were half paralyzed, but the sugar and caffeine in the soft drinks set them off again. It was 4 a.m. before they got to sleep. Not exactly a Spartan baseball regimen.

We were, by the way, the last of the eight competing teams to arrive in Williamsport. Later, we learned that the players from the Philippines had been there, resting up and practicing, for six days.

If our spirits soared on seeing the stadium, they fizzled again on seeing the compound in which the teams were housed. For the next week, we would be living in log-type cabins, one to a team, that appeared to have been built around the time the Quakers came to Pennsylvania. I half expected William Penn to greet us at the door.

In another charming throwback to yesteryear, there were no bathrooms in the cabins. Instead, there were outhouses. If the call came in the middle of the night, you staggered from the cabin and groped through the darkness for the outhouse door (or for the mess hall, where there was a bathroom).

This proved to be too difficult a trip for our young gladiators, and night after night I was awakened by a tinkling sound on the outer wall of the cabin. Outrageous, I thought.

By the end of the week, I was doing it myself. Ah, wilderness!

Larry and I had a separate room, but unlike in San Bernardino, we did not even have a door to close. Instead, there was a drop cloth, like something out of "The Road to Morocco." There was never a way for us to escape the kids. For the next week, we heard every thing they said and did. It almost made me crazy!

The kids had the same style bunk beds as in San Bernardino, but I think Little League had hired creak-installers to make the beds extra creaky. The kids would just settle down in the evening, when one bed would creak, then another and another. Soon, there was an orchestra of creaking bunk beds. Just like San Bernardino.

We were told that after the World Series, the cabins would be torn down and modern dormitories would be built in time for next year's eight teams. That did not mean a thing to us. We weren't even thinking about next year. Even if we were, chances of a team coming back two years in a row were equal to my chances of being named chairman of the Joint Chiefs of Staff.

After falling asleep at 4, we were awakened by our uncles at 7. It was Sunday, but if we'd had any hopes of sleeping in, they immediately disappeared. The uncles said there were things to be done, including physicals that each player was required to have before being allowed to play.

Why not give the physicals before sending the kids to Williamsport, I wondered? In the shadow of Little League headquarters, however, you learn not to question things. Going up against the L.L. brass is like going up against the Catholic Church, the Miss America panel of judges and the Kiwanis International.

Sunday's schedule included a photo session, an informational meeting, and an umpires' meeting. Amazingly, all three had been scheduled for the same time. In addition, there were 8,000 other things we were supposed to do. And we were still wiped out from the trip.

A lot of the team parents arrived Sunday, some having to fight for hotel rooms. Many were staying in the City View Motel, located on a high hill overlooking Lamade Stadium. You can watch a game from any room in the place. It's like having a box at the finish line of the Kentucky Derby. These were the rooms the San Ramon parents had reserved.

We heard they lost $2,000 in deposits. How sweet that was! Pardon my vindictiveness.

The meeting with the umpire in charge was dreadful. It was Sy and San Bernardino all over again. He was an elderly gentleman, a sort of militant Methuselah. He acted as if he hated to be there, but even worse, hated our being there. People were afraid to ask him a question. If you did, he looked at you as if you were subversive.

He gathered us around and explained rules you would not believe. As was the case in San Bernardino, they included rules to cover situations that will never occur between now and the end of our planet.

I was pleased to see that the Sunflower Seed Rule was also prominent in Williamsport. I had developed a whimsical fondness for the rule that outlawed sunflower seeds on the field, and I had a mental image of nefarious low-lifes in trenchcoats hanging around the outhouses and trying to sell sunflower seeds to our kids.

Obviously, Little League must protect the health and safety of the kids. But sometimes I think they go too far. The real concern about sunflower seeds, I think, is that a kid might accidentally swallow one on the field and that they might be confronted not only with a lawsuit, but a public relations disaster. Imagine holding up ABC's coverage of the final game while someone administers the Heimlich maneuver to a 12-year-old.

In my entire life, I have not heard of anyone dying from a sunflower seed. Gum, possibly, but not sunflower seeds.

In case you are wondering, yes, there was a similar rule barring the use of chewing gum. This was a bit odd since one of the sponsors of the Little League World Series was Bubblicious gum.

I particularly remember Methuselah's monologue on one rule—and I hope this never happens in a game in which I am involved. He took us out to the left field foul pole, and said something like this:

"If a fielder is going after a fly ball and his glove is over the fence in fair territory and he catches the ball but his momentum causes his glove to hit the fence and the ball pops out of his glove and lands in foul territory on the other side of the fence, it is a foul ball."

Say what?

I challenged him. "Wait a minute. Once the ball goes around the fair side of the foul pole, it's a fair ball. It doesn't matter where it lands."

Clearly, he wanted to burn me at the stake. Instead, he said philosophically, "That's the way it is in Williamsport. You're wrong, son. Next question."

The only purpose to some of the rules seemed to be to give the umpires a better chance to throw a manager, coach or player out of a game. Like the Shirttail Rule. If a kid did not have his shirt tucked in, he could be ejected. First errant shirttail, he got a warning. Second, he was out of the game. It was like baseball in a penal colony.

To this day, I do not know how umpires are chosen for the Williamsport games. They come from around the world, and although some do not speak English, they turned out to be surprisingly good umpires—certainly far better than we had in San Bernardino.

Among the umpires was a guy, Dennis Graham, from the U.S. military community in Germany. I could hardly conceal my joy on discovering that he was originally from Long Beach. As it turned out, Graham was much too fair-minded. And he wasn't allowed to umpire our games anyway.

The most memorable discovery of the day, however, had nothing to do with umpires.

Almost from the first light of Sunday morning, we noticed that the kids from the Philippines and Dominican Republic were bigger than those from the other six teams. Really bigger. The Dominicans and Filipinos were to the rest of the kids what Kareem Abdul-Jabbar (a former Little Leaguer) is to Danny DeVito (another former Little Leaguer).

We mentioned this to the people administering the physicals. They responded with smirks that confirmed our suspicions. There was no way those kids were 12 or under.

The difference was hormonal, too. There is a white fence that surrounds the compound. We later noticed the Dominicans hanging on it and ogling the girls and women passing by. Meanwhile, our kids were farther back in the compound, playing ping pong and hitting each other in the head. They had as much interest in girls as in quantum physics. Except, of course, for the King of Romance, Alex DeFazio.

Come to think of it, there were these little girl groupies, 12 years old or so, from the Williamsport area, who were forever running around our guys and asking for their autographs. Our kids did not respond very much to that. They just weren't into the birds and bees yet.

Almost everyone, including some Williamsporters, were having a good laugh over the size of the Filipinos and Dominicans. There were even jokes, such as: "Is that their pitcher or their bus driver?" Or: "Their best player had to stay home. His wife is having a baby."

These guys looked as if they did razor commercials. It was obvious to everyone that these kids were overage. Obvious, that is, to everyone except Little League headquarters.

Williamsport is a town of 32,000 people, located in north central Pennsylvania on the west branch of the Susquehanna River. You could, I suppose, put a canoe in the water there and paddle it to the Baseball Hall of Fame at Cooperstown, New York, also on the Susquehanna.

At the turn of the century, it was quite a town, a center of the lumber industry. It gave rise to a series of mansions, which exist today under the guise of a tourist attraction called "Millionaires' Row."

When the lumber ran out, so did the lumber barons. Nothing of great consequence occurred there until June 6, 1939, when a baseball team named Lundy Lumber defeated Lycoming Dairy by a score of 23 to 6. It was the first Little League game in history.

The field is still there on the edge of town, and you can go out and stand on the very mound where the Lycoming Dairy pitcher got hammered on that day way back when.

The league began with three teams and was organized by Carl Stotz and the Bebble brothers, George and Bert.

Stotz, who died two months before the 1992 World Series, was regarded as something of a saint by some of Williamsport's old-timers. At the drop of a bat, they will tell you that he was pushed aside in 1955 by a court order filed by the U.S. Rubber Company. Initially recruited by Stotz to help finance Little League, U.S. Rubber saw public relations potential in the organization.

Things got bigger—and dirtier—through the years. Stotz spoke ill of U.S. Rubber (and for a time dreamed of starting a rival league). Later, George Bebble spoke ill of Stotz, claiming the latter never acknowledged the contributions of the Brothers Bebble. And Little League Baseball, Inc., spoke of Stotz hardly at all. (He gets a dollop of mention, however, in the Little League Museum next to Little League headquarters.)

Governed for three decades by the late Peter J. McGovern, a U.S. Rubber public relations official, Little League Baseball, Inc., is now under the direction of Dr. Creighton J. Hale, a physiologist who runs the organization with the personality of an ill-tempered cherub.

I want to say something here about one of our guys simply because he deserves a mention and, despite an unlucky streak, was as much a part of the team as anyone.

Chris Miller, one of the twins, became Mr. Unlucky. When it was all over and the stats were tallied up, we found Chris had batted only .105 in 19 times at the plate. It was amazing; time after time, he would hit the ball hard, but unfortunately right at one of the fielders.

An 11-year-old, Chris never dreamed he would come back for another Little League World Series. For that matter, neither did any of us.

Each team was also scheduled for a Sunday practice session. Ours began in the late afternoon, and it lasted almost up to the opening ceremonies Sunday night. Play would begin on Monday.

The ceremony was one of the highlights of my week —no, make that my life. It was great to stand on the field in Lamade Stadium (named after a farmer who donated the land) with our kids and others from all over the world.

The stands were packed. They had a great entertainment program, including fireworks. The kids on the field and the people in the stands joined in singing "It's a Small World," and each player was given a medal in recognition of the tremendous achievement of making it to the finals in Williamsport.

Also, it was a bit of Little League history in the making. For the first time ever, they turned on the lights at Lamade Stadium. (This year's championships would include night games for the first time, a real break for our guys who had played most of their games at night.)

The anthems of the representative countries were played, and kids from the teams took turns reciting, in their native language, the Little League pledge: "I trust in God. I love my country and will respect its laws. I will play fair and strive to win, but win or lose, I will always do my best."

After the kid from the Dominican Republic finished reciting it, David Gonzalez was consumed with excitement. David is bilingual, and he turned to me with a quizzical look.

"What's wrong, David?" I asked.

"Jeff, you're not going to believe this. They have the same pledge we have."

We left the stadium right after getting our medals. Our first game was scheduled for eleven o'clock Monday morning against the U.S. Central team from South Holland, Illinois. Going on only three hours of sleep from the night before, we would need to get up in time for a pre-game practice session. In the cabin, we set the clock for 6 a.m.

Which, of course, is 3 a.m., Pacific Coast Time.

eleven

RANDALL SHELLEY

Height: 5'6"
Weight: 120

With a batting average of .429, center fielder Randall was among the strongest hitters on the team. He hit his second solo home run in the Western Regionals against defending champion San Ramon Valley. Not only an exceptional baseball player. Randall was also a standout on the soccer field—and he kept the team laughing.

We wanted to be the champions of the United States. That was our goal.

The world championship? As defeatist as it may sound, I was pretty well convinced there was no way that could happen.

Almost anyone involved with Little League in the United States in 1992 (except those at headquarters) would have understood this. It was virtually out of the question for a U.S. team to win the world championship. The international teams were usually so good, so big, and, probably, so old that they could not be beaten. You cannot put 11- and 12-year-olds up against kids of 14, 15, or even older and expect to win.

Yet that is precisely what Little League headquarters had condoned through the years. International teams had long taken advantage of the fact that rules regarding proof of age were much more relaxed in their countries. It was pretty much up to the district director to decide which kids were eligible. Moreover, there wasn't a lot of record keeping in some of those countries. You're talking about kids who were not always born in hospitals with an army of clerks to document the event. U.S. kids, on the other hand, were governed by strict rules regarding proof of age and residence.

Those countries had other advantages as well. For example, the Philippines team had ended its regular season back in March or April. They had about four months off before they had to play Taiwan for the Far East title.

The record reflected all this one-sidedness. Since 1968, when the L.L. World Series became a truly international event, Asian teams had won it 19 times. U.S. teams had won it five times. Asians had won in seven of the last eight years.

Why did Little League brass allow this to happen? Probably because they did not want to discourage foreign teams from playing. They had made the international game, on Saturday, the final day, the premier event of Little League World Series week. It was the game that for years had been broadcast by ABC-TV, and that meant more bucks for the Little League treasury.

Without that final international game, the L.L. chiefs may have thought ABC would lose interest. Personally, I think TV viewers would be more interested in the national game, one U.S. team against another. (The national game is played on Thursday of each World Series week and is broadcast by ESPN.)

All this is by way of explaining why we had limited our sights to winning the U.S. championship. But that would not be easy either. The word had gotten around that the Central team was tough. And that the Eastern team was even tougher.

By Sunday afternoon, our league president, Bill Marshall, and District 38 director Bob McKittrick had already gotten Long Beach involved in a minor fracas with Little League headquarters.

Throughout All-Star play, our kids had worn the initials "R.G." on their uniforms as a tribute to Ruben Gutierrez, the umpire killed in June. But the brass at L.L. headquarters was questioning whether the kids would be allowed to wear the initials in Lamade Stadium. They made some explanation about the uniforms of all the teams needing to be...well, uniform.

Fine, I could understand that. But, instead of saying flat out that we could not use the initials, headquarters delayed, stringing us out for a day or two. We had team moms waiting with needle and thread at the ready. Little League waited until after the first game before making its "no" official.

Playing at Williamsport was a bit like playing at Wimbledon. There was a dress code. Managers and coaches had to wear long pants. During the All-Star season, Larry and I always wore short pants. It was Reason Number 56 for why we live in Southern California.

I had to go out and buy trousers. Black polyester trousers that were hot as all get-out.

Larry had brought trousers, but, having picked up a few pounds during All-Star play, discovered he could not buckle his belt. He tried to cover the problem with his shirt, but was reminded (how could he have forgotten?) that this was a gross offense. In the end, he slit his trousers slightly in the rear in order to get into them. They don't cover this sort of thing in the Little League instruction manual.

The kids were having trouble adjusting to outhouse discipline. Steve Warshauer visited the compound, and he had to go to the bathroom.

"C'mon, Dad, I'll show you where it is," said Jeff.

He took his father outside. And led him to a tree.

By the time we went home, I think we left a few dead trees behind.

Our game against Central Monday morning was the first of the tournament. Since we were the last team to arrive, this seemed a tad unfair. (I was becoming a world-class whiner.) It would have been more equitable to have the first game played by two of the international teams that had arrived days earlier.

We had a warm-up drill that morning. It helped to loosen up the kids, but there were problems. Since Dane Mayfield's arm had gone kaput in the Hawaii game, Sean had become our hottest pitcher. After that, it was Ryan Beaver and Randall Shelley.

At practice, however, Sean did not look sharp. Nor did our hitters. I think it had a lot to do with jet lag and with the fact that, Pacific Time, the game was starting at 8 a.m. Our kids simply were not ready.

Central's pitcher did not throw that hard, but neither did our guys hit very hard. It was one of those games in which we could not seem to get anything going. After three innings, we had a 1-1 tie.

U.S. Champs, Part Two: Umpire (exiting photo) barely has time to flee before team begins celebrating its second consecutive U.S. championship. Player with upraised arm and seeming to be posing for statue is Brent Kirkland. (Alex Garcia /Press-Telegram)

Bad Bounce: In the 1993 championship game, Panama's Onesimo Morales slides safely into third as an errant throw skips past Brent Kirkland. Morales scored on the play to put Panama up 2-1, but that was the last run the Latin Americans would score. (Hillary Sloss / Press-Telegram)

Heroes' Welcome: Jeffrey Warshauer and Ali Strain-Bay glide through the streets of Long Beach during the 1992 U.S. championship victory parade. This was a few days before we were given the world title. (Alex Garcia / Press-Telegram)

Saint Alex? In what appears to be a prayerful posture at Williamsport, Alex DeFazio, the Don Juan of the All-Stars, is actually focusing on the batter. Or maybe a babe in the stands. (Hillary Sloss / Press-Telegram)

Haircuts Are Not Us: Larry on the right, yours truly on the left, share a quiet moment with Brady Lewis during tournament play in California. By then, nearly all of us needed a barbershop. (Alex Garcia / Press-Telegram)

World Champs! The dugout empties after Jeremy Hess drives in the winning run against Panama. That guy on the left resembling the Incredible Hulk is Sean. (Alex Garcia / Press-Telegram)

Flying Jeremy: I scoop up Jeremy after his hit wins us the 1993 World championship. Luckily, I stopped myself from instinctively throwing him to second base. (Alex Garcia / Press-Telegram)

That's My Boy: Sean dances off the mound after his no-hit performance helped our guys win the 1993 U.S. championship in Williamsport.
(Hillary Sloss / Press-Telegram)

Little League's Field of Dreams: This is what Williamsport's Howard J. Lamade Stadium looks like to those who come early and get the good seats on the hill beyond the outfield. (Alex Garcia / Press-Telegram)

Then, in the top of the fourth, we exploded for six runs, helped by a three-run homer from Kevin Sullivan. I thought what you should never think in baseball: "Well, this game is over."

Something happens to baseball kids at that age; they get big leads and suddenly let down a bit. They don't concentrate as much. It happened to our kids. Illinois roared back in the bottom of the fourth, and before I knew it, we had a slim 7-6 lead and they had two men on base. Happily, Sean struck out the next two batters.

We came back with three more runs. Final score, 10-6. It had not been an easy game.

A few minutes later, back at the compound, you would not have known our guys had been in a ball game. They were in the pool or playing ping-pong or eating or trading pins.

They were getting to know some of the other kids and were having fun trying to crack the language barrier. One of the Dominicans, a really nice kid, virtually demolished the barrier. A pin-trader who knew no English, he was always after our guys, always trying to bargain them out of pins. The kid was amazing. I look for him to be Secretary General of the United Nations some day.

The kids tended to mix more than the adults. We had some contact with the other managers and coaches, but not much. We'd practice by ourselves and eat in our own little chosen spots in the cafeteria.

One of our little guys was getting to know—or trying to get to know—one of Williamsport's little girls. Walking past Alex at one point while he chatted with the young lady, I shuddered on hearing something about "my mother's motel room."

And something else about "coming over to see my pin collection."

When all this is over, I thought, maybe we could get Alex some new lines.

By now, a real media crunch was developing. Although I had been a major-league MVP, a member of the All-Star team a couple of times, and on the Toronto team that won a division title, I'd never seen anything like the media phenomenon that blossomed around our kids.

Part of it was a fascination some of the media had for the story of a former major leaguer coaching his son's Little League team. There were a lot of requests for interviews with Sean and me. (I could not know it then, but it was a mere warm-up for what would come the following year. I will have more to say elsewhere about what all this meant to me and Sean, as father and son.)

There were no phones inside the cabins. Anyone trying to call us had to go through a command post. An operator would take the message, then pass it to the uncles, who would post it in the barracks. There were stacks of messages from media people who wanted us to phone them back.

To me, there is no reason to be inundated by the media when you are 11 or 12 years old. Also, I was terrified one of our kids would say something enormously embarrassing—you know, one of those devastating things that would wind up on blooper records for decades to come.

At first, the kids liked the media attention. But they tired of it after a couple of days and became adept at avoiding media people. When they saw them coming, they'd turn around and head the other way (as if apprenticing for a major-league career).

Still, there were some interviews. After every game, managers and coaches had to go to a tent where there was a microphone and a stand. The media would then grill us as if we were conducting the Persian Gulf War.

Now and then, I found myself saying, "Hold on, guys. These are little babies out here, little 11- and 12-year-olds. Sure, there is strategy in their games—but it isn't quite as intense as it is in the Bigs."

In short, we tried not to let the media get carried away. I think some of them were aspiring sportswriters and this was their training ground. They were asking questions they would be asking big-league managers. We learned to use up a lot of the time by joking and kidding around with them.

This was the first year in which Little League had instituted "pool play" in the World Series. It used to be that if you lost one game, you were out of the tournament. But now, every U.S. team played every other U.S. team at least once, and the teams with the best records squared off for the national title.

On Tuesday, we played the East—the All Stars from the Nottingham Little League, Hamilton Square, New Jersey. Once again, it was not easy.

Ryan Stuart hit a homer in the top of the first, and we shut them out for a couple of innings. But in the bottom of the third, just as we were starting to think we had overrated them, they bombed us with four runs.

A six-inning Little League game is a bit like Thanksgiving dinner. Both can go by pretty quickly. A ground ball here and a pop-up there—next thing you know, the game is over. So here we were. Halfway through this game and behind 4 to 1.

The top of the fourth, however, we started hitting. The hero of the game, without a doubt, was Alex. Now, Alex coming up to bat looked about as threatening as Little Boy Blue. He weighed about 70 pounds, and there are dogs taller than he is. Moreover, he had not shown any power in the game against Illinois.

So when Alex came up in the fourth, the East manager looked like a windmill as he frantically waved in his outfield. It was just like in a movie. On the very next pitch, Alex slammed a fastball over the left fielder's head for a triple. By the end of the inning, we were ahead, 5 to 4. We stayed ahead, adding one more run while Ryan Beaver shut down the East.

It was an amazing game. Beav had played practically every day for two months before going into the World Series. His fastball wasn't lively, his curve wasn't breaking sharply, his control was off.

Result: He threw a one-hitter. But he walked 10 guys.

Now this is the sort of thing that sends coaches to the coronary wing of the nearest hospital. When you walk 10 men in one game, you are not supposed to win. Beav had not even walked that many men total, all year. But he started every inning of this game by walking someone, as if that were one of the rules of the game. Still, he made the big pitch when it counted.

Dane Mayfield got into this game. His arm had swelled so badly that he had not played since the Hawaii game in San Bernardino. We put him in as a pinch-hitter with two outs. He got a base hit up the middle and drove in a run.

Our kids had gotten a little steamed during the game. When the East players slid, it appeared as if they were trying to trip our basemen. That fit with something I had noticed while scouting them in an earlier game. In that contest, when they hit a grounder and were thrown out at first, they seemed to go out of their way to step on the first baseman—right on his heel, on the Achilles tendon. I saw this happen a couple of times.

Amazingly, the umpires let them get away with this. Maybe if one of their guys had run down to first and stepped on the baseman's foot while eating a sunflower seed, he would have been thrown out of the game.

Also, they did a weird thing with flash cards. I never fully understood it. Somebody in the dugout would hold up a card—actually, bigger than a card—with bizarre writing on it, like hieroglyphics. It looked like a bad half-time card show at a football game.

We weren't sure what it was all about, but we questioned it anyway, going all the way to Joe Lausch, the tournament director. We said something absolutely brilliant like, "They can't do whatever it is they're doing."

Amazingly, he agreed. The East stopped using flash-cards in the dugout. Instead, they used them from the stands.

Kids as young as Little Leaguers have the attention span of a gnat. Every now and then, Larry and I would have a little trouble getting the kids interested in the game in which they were taking part.

They'd be goofing off in the dugout, slapping each other around and so on, and one of us would have to say something like, "Gee, we hate to interrupt your fun with something as unimportant as baseball. But since you may not have noticed, we thought we'd call your attention to the fact that we're losing this game."

That was usually enough to bring the kids to their feet and get them back into the game—as cheerleaders as well as players.

Almost every team that gets to Williamsport has three or four exceptional players. But I had scouted practice sessions of the teams from the Philippines and the Dominican Republic, and I came away with the unsettling discovery that each had 14 exceptional players. Their worst player would have been one of our best.

They were strong, smooth, and big. They had great arms and terrific speed. Time after time, I saw Dominican outfielders grab fly balls off the fence, turn around, and throw line drive strikes from right field to third, or left field to home plate on the fly. These included guys who were not even on the starting team.

Twelve-year-olds? No way.

The Filipinos were smaller than the Dominicans, but Filipinos are not a very big people. They, too, had great arms, and never missed a ball that came to them. I thought they looked like 18-year-olds. Little did I know then how right I was.

Watching them reinforced the goal we had set going to Williamsport. I told Larry, "We have to zero in on the national championship because the game after it will be rough. I dread facing the Philippine or Dominican team. I love our kids so much that I don't want to see them get beat 20 to 0 on national television. They might never want to play baseball again."

As if to prove my point, the Dominicans beat the European team, 24 to 0. The game was called after five innings. (The European players were actually Americans, the sons of people serving with the U.S. military in Germany.)

Meanwhile, the Philippines beat Canada, 12 to 0, but had a tougher time than the score indicated. Canada threw a lefthander against them, and the kids from the Philippine city of Zamboanga had some trouble with him.

A long time before our All-Star season began, the parents of one of our players had separated. But we were out on the field one day, and I happened to look at the stands. There they were. It was not a reconciliation, but it was kind of neat to see them put aside their differences for the duration of the Williamsport games.

On Wednesday, we played the South team, and I don't think kids ever played under more difficult circumstances than those boys from Lake Charles, Louisiana. At game time, Hurricane Andrew was closing in on their town. They played that whole game while worrying if their houses would be there when they got home. As it turned out, the hurricane made a sudden turn and missed Lake Charles by about 100 miles.

Perhaps more than any story I know, this illustrates the importance some people place on Little League. For some time, the Lake Charles team had known the hurricane was heading their way. Still, they turned their backs on it, picked up their gear, and headed for Williamsport.

In fact, they were the most true-grit team of the tournamont. Their pitcher, Ryan Zembower, was a kid who had, four or five years earlier, lost an eye.

The Southern team really had my admiration.

That day, before the game against the South, Rod Shelley had a dream. He went around sharing it with other parents. In his dream, Randall, his son, pitched against the South. Our guys won by a lopsided score of 16 to 1.

In real life, Randall did pitch. He was cool. You'd think a kid not used to pitching would be nervous in front of 18,000 or so fans. But Randall's adrenaline was really flowing. After warming him up, our catcher, Jeff War-shauer, came back and said, "Coach, he looks better than anybody we have. He's really throwing well, hitting the corners and keeping the ball down. He just looks great."

Jeff knew what he was talking about. Randall allowed only two or three hits. He did not walk a man.

As if the South did not have enough to worry about with Hurricane Andrew, the game was played under the lights. And I don't think they were used to playing at night back home.

When we saw we were going to win, I did what I could to hold up runners at third and keep the score down. I've been on the losing side and know how badly you can feel by being clobbered. Nevertheless, the final score was—

You guessed it. 16 to 1.

The South people were every bit as gracious as southerners are famous for being. Their manager, Steve Manuel, came over to us at the end of the game and said we were the best team he ever had seen. Just hearing him say that was almost as good as winning the national championship.

But not quite.

The only undefeated U.S. team, we were now one game and one day away from our national championship goal. The game for the U.S. title would put us up against the U.S. team with the second-best record.

Second best turned out to be the Eastern team from Hamilton Square, New Jersey.

twelve

MICHAEL HOLDEN

Height: 5'5"
Weight: 115

Although 1992 was only his third
year in baseball, Michael showed
exceptional fundamental talents
and speed. As an all-star, he batted
.286 and hit one memorable
home run. He came to the all-stars
from the regular-season Dodgers.

Back home in Long Beach, people were going crazy. You almost had to have lived in the city a few years to understand why.

Long Beach had been having a tough time. Its naval station, a fixture since before World War II, was about to be closed, along with another long-time military installation, the Long Beach Navy Hospital. Thousands of people had been laid off by the city's largest employer, the aircraft firm of McDonnell Douglas Corporation. The Disney Company, after a lot of talk about building a new theme park in the city, had picked up its blueprints and walked away. The much-publicized riots that had swept through Los Angeles earlier in the year had ravaged Long Beach as well, causing millions of dollars in damage.

Add to all that a tremendous crime and gang problem, and you have the portrait of a city creeping toward the edge of despair.

Then suddenly, along came this baseball team of 11- and 12-year-olds who did what politicians, preachers and psychologists could not do. They got the people of Long Beach to feel good about their city. And, more importantly, about themselves.

In addition to front-page stories on the All-Stars, the *Long Beach Press-Telegram* was urging readers to get behind the team. Makeshift signs were showing up on front lawns and in windows. A restaurant on the west side of town had started posting stories of our early victories and players. By the time we were done, the stories covered an entire wall. Although the Williamsport games were not yet on TV, you could dial the local cable station and hear an audio broadcast direct from Pennsylvania. The *Press-Telegram* initiated a phone line for readers to call to get the inning-by-inning scores. Around the third day, the phone line broke down from too many calls.

In Williamsport, we were getting telegrams of support and even gifts, such as homemade Little League necklaces sent to the team moms by a Long Beacher named Noreen Evans.

Before playing the East for the U.S. title, we received a call from John Morris, a civic booster and restaurant owner in Long Beach.

"Win or lose," he said, "we're going to have one heck of a downtown parade for the kids."

The U.S. championship game began Thursday at 5 p.m. It was still early afternoon in Long Beach, but a big portion of the city's commerce virtually came to a halt. People were having Little League TV parties. The bars, especially the sports bars, were jammed.

Sean was going to pitch. To me, this was the consummate game. The teams consisted of legal players. It meant much more to me than that impending Saturday farce in which the players from the Philippines, now the international champions, not only were so obviously illegal, but had a tacit sanction from the officials at Little League headquarters.

It was not that the U.S. championship was a big deal to just Larry and me. It was a big deal to anyone in the U.S. who really understood how Little League works. They knew that in the U.S., you just cannot cheat. The competition and jealousies between various Little Leagues, even among people in your own town, are so great that if one kid lives 10 feet outside the boundaries or is one day overage, someone will somehow find out and turn him in.

That's the way it is from Maine to California. If you are on a U.S. team that winds up in Williamsport, you are legitimate. By the time you get that far, you've been checked and double-checked by all sorts of folks.

That, to me, is what makes the U.S. championship contest *the* game of the annual Little League week in Williamsport. I only wish the media saw it that way and gave the U.S. game more of its due. Maybe someday they'll might make that the big, ABC-televised game on Saturday.

Nervous? Of course I was. But being nervous did not mean a thing compared to another problem: Some of the kids had gotten the flu.

"Little League Flu," we started calling it. A kid would get deathly ill for about 12 hours, then be okay. There was some speculation that the European champs brought it from Germany. Their kids were so sick that for a time it looked as if they would not be able to field a team.

It had taken a toll also among the Canadian players from Quebec, and then it somehow reached the little ol' cabin of the West.

One of our guys, Michael Holden, was sick as a dog. In addition to our not having an indoor bathroom, there weren't even trash cans in the cabins. That meant the only place a kid could upchuck was on the floor. I will spare you the details of what this did to sanitary conditions there.

Barbara Holden was staying at the City View, so we thought it would be better for Michael to stay there, where she could nurse him and he would not spread the flu to others. Since this plan made a great deal of sense, the Little League officials naturally would not permit it. They invoked the hard, fast rule that, no matter what, all players must stay within the compound.

Even the doctor and nurse hired by Little League adhered to the rule. Until Michael threw up on them.

Well, almost on them. They were coming out of the mess hall, and Michael, about 20 feet away, let loose like the possessed kid in *The Exorcist*. The nurse, who up to that point had not even seen him, said, "Gosh, you're right. The little guy is pretty sick."

So Michael was at last excused and allowed to pass through the hallowed portals of the City View Motel.

Next, David Gonzalez came down with the flu. Jeff Warshauer also got it and still had it when he went out and caught for the national championship game.

ESPN was televising the national title game; it was exciting to know we were on the tube across the land. I gave the kids my usual Knute Rockne pre-game talk in which, among other things, I said, "This is the most important game of your life."

It was, in fact, our 21st game as a team. I had given essentially the same speech 21 times.

The East had a fine pitcher named Matt Wolski. The son of the team's coach, he played shortstop when he wasn't pitching, and he was a superb ballplayer. But the East had gotten itself into a jam in its last game against Central U.S. To get out of it, they put Wolski on the mound for two innings. Per Little League rules, that made him ineligible to pitch the next day against us. It was a real break for our guys. But it also may have made us a bit cocky. There was a real sense that we were going to clobber the kids from New Jersey.

We did not. The East pitched a boy named Adam Fomoso on the mound. He had not pitched at all in Williamsport. From what we saw at the start of the game, he did not throw hard and all he really had was a dinky little curveball. I started to think, "We're going to kill this guy."

But Fomoso turned out to be amazing. He had great control and was hitting the inside corner of the plate, which is what the East coach, Matt Wolski Sr., liked his kids to do. Good for Wolski. You don't see many Little League coaches or managers do that because they're afraid of their pitcher hitting the batters.

The short of it was that we could not seem to get a run. Ground ball here, pop-up there. Fomoso did not strike out many of our guys, but his team had great defense. We went through five innings of what became a monumental struggle and still there was no score.

In the front row of the stands, John Beaver and his brother, Joe, were wearing the most hideous caps in the history of headwear. They were manufactured in a series of awful fluorescent colors that became more awful as they faded. To make the appearance even worse, at the top of the fifth inning, the Brothers Beaver reversed the hats, wearing them in rally fashion.

Get the Hollywood scriptwriters ready. In the top of the sixth inning, with his father and uncle making perfect fools of themselves in the stands, Ryan Beaver came to bat.

On an 0-1 count and swinging late, Beav drilled a ball to right field.

It was one of those baseball moments when time seems to slow to about a hundredth of its normal speed. I can still see the ball suspended over right field, still feel the silence of more than 20,000 people waiting to see where it would go.

It went over the fence—just barely in fair territory.

Maybe it curved around the foul pole before leaving the stadium, but I didn't think so. Still, I wondered. In the coach's box, I thought, "I know it's fair. And Ryan is running, so he knows it's fair. But will the umpires know it's fair?" These are the kinds of calls umpires blow all the time—plus I was thinking back to the chief umpire who thought a ball curving around the foul pole was a foul ball.

But the umpire stuck his arm out. Fair ball.

We were ahead, 1 to 0.

In the stands, John Beaver, on the edge of a stroke, turned about the color of his dumb cap. He also had tears streaming down his cheeks, as did his wife, Linda.

Sean retired the next three batters. The Long Beach All-Stars were the Little League champions of the United States.

People watching the game on television said later that we did not look all that excited. If only they knew.

Maybe I did not leap for joy myself because I was afraid that doing so would trigger a heart attack. My blood pressure was ready to explode. I almost had to be helped out of the dugout.

In the stands, people were chanting, "U-S-A! U-S-A!" Even the Eastern fans were doing it. It was a very classy thing for them to do; their way of wishing us well against the international champs on Saturday.

I never did find out what the television ratings were for that national championship game, but I suspect they were better than the ratings for Saturday's game. I know that if I had turned on the Thursday game, I would have watched it.

Heaven forgive me. I hoped that, back in California, Chickie Walsh was watching.

Delighted as the Long Beach contingent was, one of our parents had mixed feelings about the victory. William Stuart, Ryan's father, had a fine, patriarchal beard. Somewhere along the way during the All-Star season, Ryan had idly asked him, "Dad, if we win the national championship, will you shave off your beard?"

William said what any father, half paying attention, would say under the circumstances.

"Yeah, yeah, sure."

After the game, I did what some of the other parents thought was a strange thing. I went off on my own for a couple of hours.

Emotionally, I was drained. So, I think, was everyone else on the team. We had all shed a few tears after the U.S. championship game, which was one of the greatest games I've ever seen.

I made it back for the poolside victory party the parents were having at a nearby motel. But even then I wanted to be away from everything and everyone. I wanted to just savor our accomplishment. We had done the incredible thing, the once-in-a-lifetime thing that, only a few weeks ago, we had not even dared talk about.

Mentally, I also was tottering back and forth between being a coach and a father. First, we had won the national championship. Second, we had won it with my son, Sean, pitching. He had given up three hits, struck out nine, and pitched his sixth or seventh shutout of All-Star play.

My own field of dreams had come true.

In the Long Beach area, people were in a frenzy. Rightfully so. It was even more exciting than the big-league World Series that would take place in a few weeks.

Among other things, people were planning the parade, set for Tuesday of the following week. They were organizing TV parties for Saturday's game and even reserving seats in bars.

As he had done in San Bernardino, Larry still checked in daily with his law firm back in California. As I noted, it is a big firm—30 or 40 lawyers, plus about another 60 staff people. After a while, it got so they wanted Larry to call in at a certain time every day. The phone would ring and someone would run through the office like Paul Revere, yelling, "It's Larry! It's Larry!"

Ten or 15 guys would head for the conference room. Larry would be put on the speaker, and for the next half hour they would drill him. Why didn't he pinch-hit so-and-so in yesterday's game? Who was going to pitch on Saturday? And on and on.

Now and then, someone in the firm would ask Larry, "Do you want to know what's going on with such-and-such a case?"

Larry would answer "Only if it's absolutely essential."

Earlier in the day, in what I called the Battle of the Grown-Ups, the Philippines had beaten the Dominican Republic. This surprised some people because, while the Filipinos were big, the Dominicans were even bigger. Steve Warshauer thought they were a major-league farm team that had gotten lost.

In a way, they were sort of a farm team. The Dominican kids were from the Epy Guerrero Little League in Santo Domingo. Epy Guerrero is a scout for the Toronto Blue Jays, my last major-league team. The Blue Jays are said to have contributed a lot of money to help the Dominican Little League.

One of the zillion rumors swirling around the compound was that Guerrero and Pat Gillick, the Jays general manager, would fly in, watch the final game, and sign a couple of kids to professional baseball contracts. Major-league teams have been known to sign kids 15 and 16 years old. And, clearly, the Dominicans had some kids who were 15 and 16 years old.

On one occasion, I saw some of the players from the Dominican Republic using the common shower in the compound. Anatomically speaking, they looked like managers and coaches.

For their game against the Dominican Republic, the Philippines went with their best pitcher, a kid who threw like Sandy Koufax. He even looked like Sandy Koufax. (Could it be? Nah.) By throwing to the corners of the plate virtually at will, he shut down the Dominicans, 4 to 1.

In the wake of that game, another rumor arose. The Dominican Republic, the story went, had thrown the game against the Philippines. Why? Supposedly because the Dominicans were about to be exposed for having overage players, and a victory would draw too much attention to them.

The alleged whistle-blower was a Little League manager from Mexico. His team had played the Dominican Republic earlier in the year. Reportedly, he was not saying that they had changed their roster between the time he played them and the time they arrived in Williamsport.

On our way to the airport that Sunday, the manager from Mexico's Little League hitched a ride on our bus. By then, the 1992 World Series was Little League history (or so we thought), and the guy told Larry something like this:

"The Dominican kids who played us were not the same Dominican kids who played in Williamsport. You can look at their team pictures, and see different people in the group. They added five or six players to the team before coming to Williamsport."

He claimed some players were as old as 18, although I don't know his basis for that claim.

It would be the U.S. versus the Philippines on Saturday. Having watched the Philippines practice earlier in the week, I tried to brace our parents for what was likely to happen.

"If these kids are 12, I'm Houdini," I said. "For years, the Little League people in Williamsport have permitted this annual farce in which foreign teams, usually Asian, come over here with illegal, overage players and beat our kids. It probably won't be any different this year."

In the Philippines, the original All-Star team from Zamboanga had been chosen back in January. That meant that they'd had until July to practice for their tournament games. But in that six months, they were apparently doing more than practicing. As was later revealed, they were shuffling players around the Philippines and bringing in kids who lived as far as 800 miles from Zamboanga.

Even their manager, Rodolfo Lugay, a former player supposedly known as the "Babe Ruth of the Philippines," was illegal. He was from Manila, 540 miles away.

In retrospect, it seems to me now that any media person who had done a bit of homework would have realized something was wrong. Zamboanga is 400 or 500 miles from Manila. The people in the two cities do not even speak the same dialect.

Eventually, we learned that only four kids of the original All-Stars were still on the team.

My greatest fear was that, in playing the Philippines on national TV, our kids would get slaughtered. I did not tell them that, of course. I did not want them to start thinking there was no way they could win.

But I think some of them were thinking that anyway. There were so many rumors around the compound that they knew that they would have have to play the best game they had ever played. And the Filipinos would have to play the worst game they ever played.

Back in 1987, I had seen the Northwood All-Star team from Irvine, California. They had a couple of terrific pitchers, big kids who really threw hard, and they had a tremendous offensive team. They just clobbered everyone they played. Until Williamsport, when they went up against the Hua Lien team from Taipei, Taiwan. Hua Lien won, 21 to 1. It was absolutely unbelievable.

Equally unbelievable was the fact that in the 20 years leading up to the 1992 World Series, U.S. teams had scored a total of 33 runs in the final game while the foreign teams had scored 157. That simply did not make sense.

In a way, I understood the cheating. Take an undeveloped country like the Philippines, which rarely gets many breaks and does not make much of an impact on the international scene. All of a sudden, here's a chance for one moment in the sun. So they go for it, no matter what it takes to get it.

In addition, there's the fact that they have to pay their own transportation to the U.S. That's right. As I noted earlier, Little League flies the U.S. teams to Williamsport, but it does not put up a dime of travel money for the foreign teams. Flying an entire team to the U.S. is a big investment for a country like the Philippines. They're apt to do whatever they can to see that investment pay off.

Nevertheless, it made me heartsick to think of Little League allowing that to happen over and over to American kids. No doubt it is difficult to police the foreign teams, to make certain their kids are of legal age and are from the districts they claim to be from.

With all the money at its disposal, Little League should be able to send someone out from the U.S. each year to make a tighter check on the foreign players. Send someone out to check, say, the school records of the two teams competing for the Far East title. It would not be a perfect system, but it would be better than what they had in 1992, which was almost nothing.

For years, in fact, the foreign teams never had to provide the same proof as Americans kids. Some players even got by with a signed statement from an adult of their choice, maybe something like, "I have known Ming for 20 years, and I can assure you he is only 12 years old."

Meanwhile, U.S. kids playing on All-Star teams had to show birth certificates, phone bills, water bills, finger-prints, notarized sonograms, and DNA test results.

Okay, I'm exaggerating. But you get the idea.

One of our supporters suggested we kidnap a Filipino, cut him in half, and count the rings to determine his age.

He was kidding. I think.

thirteen

RYAN STUART

Height: 5'6"
Weight: 90

This first baseman was one of the
most improved players in the
league in 1992. In a surprising
spurt, Ryan grew nearly three
inches since the previous year. This
season he was one of the better
defensive players on the team,
with seven home runs and a .386
batting average.

At the stadium Friday morning, there was a rehearsal for
the next day's opening ceremonies, which would be part of
the ABC telecast. We were required to have the kids down
there in uniform.

Jim Palmer, Brent Musburger and Julie Moran had
arrived to do the announcing. I knew Jim from my ball-
playing days, when I'd even managed to hit a few homers
off him.

Although I like Jim, I got peeved when he started
talking about how the Filipinos and Dominicans and others did so well at Williamsport because they played baseball eight hours a day, 12 months a year, and so on.

"Tell you what," I said. "You can play baseball 24
hours a day for 12 months a year, and there's still no way

you can get ballplayers this good at age 12. If there is even one player on those teams who is legal, I'd be amazed."

His reply was, "Oh, yeah, you guys always say that. You just can't admit that they're better than your players are."

With his trained eye that had seen a lot of baseball, Jim must have known there was something amiss. But he was there to do the game for ABC, who had paid for the rights to telecast the game. And that may have prevented him from saying too much.

It continues to amaze me that, through all the years, no one in the media had broken this story.

The rehearsal went off fine, with the national anthem sung by Taylor John, son of Tommy John, the former Yankee pitcher. Taylor had just had a part on Broadway as one of the scruffy street kids in "Les Misérables," and he may be the only kid in history who quit the Broadway stage in order to go home and play Little League baseball.

After the rehearsal, it rained. Really poured. Some of us had slipped away from the compound and were kicking back at the City View when suddenly there was the most ungodly scream I'd ever heard. It was around the corner and down a staircase, and it sounded as if someone had been shot or stabbed. From a coach's standpoint, what had happened was almost as bad.

Michael Holden had gotten hurt.

Shaking off the flu, he had felt well enough to leave his room. He was ascending a flight of cement steps when he fell, smashing the bridge of his nose on the edge of a step.

We called 911. From the response, I got the impression people are not too busy in Williamsport. There must have been eight cars that showed up, including those of paramedics with sirens blaring. There were stretchers. There were neck braces.

Fearing the worst, I guess, they put Michael in one of those splints in which he could not move his spinal column. They checked all his vital signs. By the time they got him into the ambulance, about 30 minutes later, he looked like a mummy with all the tape on him. His head was in a splint, he probably still had the flu, and, as X-rays would show, he had a broken nose. Michael was not having a great time.

I'm sure the incident only confirmed to Little League officials that they had been correct in opposing the plan to move Michael to the motel.

Friday was also Day One of the scandal we came to call Ticketgate.

As I mentioned earlier, there is never a charge to get into a Little League game. But for the final World Series game, you must have a ticket.

Supposedly, blocks of tickets are set aside to accomodate parents and supporters of each team. Little League headquarters distributes them to the uncles, who, in turn, pass them on to the team.

That, at least, is the way it is supposed to work.

We had told our uncles we would need about 120 tickets. They grumbled and said 60 or 70 was probably the best they could do.

"We have people who came all the way from California for this game," we said. "It would be kind of nice if they could get inside the stadium to see it."

Not only did we stick to our request for 120 tickets, but we made an end run around the uncles. Unknown to them, we went right to the person in charge of ticket distribution. He said 120 tickets would be no problem.

Dawn Shelley, Randall's mom, was handling all this for us, and she could not have done a better job. When she got our envelope from the uncles, there were only 80 tickets inside. The uncles claimed that was the number they were given. But it was obvious that between the time the envelope left the ticket office and the time it was put in Dawn's hand, it had been opened.

Dawn went after the uncles like Carry Nation tackling a saloon.

To this day, I don't quite know how she managed it, but she went to L.L. headquarters and made a presentation so forceful that the suspect uncles were summoned to the mountaintop, where they eventually admitted to lifting some tickets for local friends.

They were disgraced.

But not very disgraced. The same guys were back the following year.

Early Saturday morning, I was asked to do a couple of interviews on the field with ABC. When I returned to the barracks, Larry looked the way he might look some day if he ever loses a big case, which, of course, will never happen.

"I have bad news," he said. "Sean has the virus."

Four or five kids had spent part of Friday in the barracks throwing up. Perhaps fed up with my inefficiency as a cabin honcho, a crew of team moms came in and really cleaned up the place. They scrubbed it from top to bottom. That helped a lot, but did not quite prevent the flu bug from spreading. Now it was Sean's turn.

Sean looked awful. And felt awful, mentally and physically. The absolute culmination of any U.S. Little Leaguer's experience is to get to the World Series game against the international champion. And here was my Little Leaguer with diarrhea and throwing up every few minutes.

We sent for the doctor. He examined Sean and told him to bend over. And it was in that awkward position that my son made a bid for baseball immortality as possibly the only boy in history to play in the Little League World Series and be given a suppository on the same day.

In the wake of the incident with Michael Holden, we now knew better than to ask permission for Sean to rest at the City View Motel, where the rest of my family was staying. The officials might say no.

Without asking, we took Sean up there and told him to sleep and to come down to the stadium if he felt better.

Before every game in Williamsport, there was a coin toss in the cafeteria to determine who would be the home team. We kept emerging as the visiting team in one coin toss after another, one after another, just as we had done throughout All-Star competition.

However, the coin toss with the Philippines went the other way. We would be the home team—for the first time. In retrospect, I should have known it was a bad omen.

You could almost feel our fortunes sliding. We wanted to hold a pre-game practice that day on one of the nearby fields set aside for that purpose. But trying to do so got us embroiled in another run-in with our uncles. Williamsport was turning into World War III.

Game time was 4 p.m. Our request for a practice field earlier in the day did not seem to us like a big deal. But...

"Nope. Just can't do it," said one of our uncles.

Things got a bit ugly, and we said we were going to use a practice field with or without their permission. Eventually, they gave in. We were assigned a field that, to us, seemed precariously close to a parking area in which a lot of cars already had arrived.

There were some L.L. officials nearby, and we asked them, in view of the proximity of the cars, if we really should practice there.

"Some of our guys can hit the ball over that fence," we said.

They told us, "Go ahead, don't worry."

Still, we hesitated. After starting out by fighting to get the field, we really had misgivings about using it. But the officials were adamant.

So we began our practice, and it was not long before the inevitable happened. One of our guys tagged a ball over the fence, about 250 feet away. Since there were cars parked right on the other side of the fence, it was hardly surprising when we heard the crash of breaking glass. One windshield gone. Still, the officials did not stop us.

Now, it is not often that a kid in the presence of adults—or, in the case of Larry, Denny and me, pseudo-adults—can break a window and get away with it. I think our kids would have stayed there for a week. Sensing an opportunity that would never come again in their lifetimes, they began swinging for the fences—actually, the windows.

It was like hitting goldfish bowls at a county fair. Every ball that went out of that practice field hit a car—and, in three or four cases, they hit car windows, which prompted the kids to jump up and down in ecstasy.

If we could have arranged for cars to be parked on the other side of the stadium fence for the game, things might have turned out very differently.

This was the last practice we would have as a team. Thank heavens. The months of practices had been fine for the kids, but they had finally taken a toll on the adults.

Al Huntley had a bruise on his leg about the size of Long Beach's most famous landmark, the *Queen Mary*. Mike Sullivan had a lump on his head from a ball that hit him while he was helping during infield practice. I had a bruised shoulder. Larry was exhausted. And every adult pitching arm was dead from one batting practice too many. Chad Stuart's 70-mph practice-session fastball was down to a tepid 40 mph.

Chad was done. All the adults were done. You could have stuck a fork in us.

At that last practice, we had brought in Ira Strain-Bay, Ali's older brother, to throw to the kids.

By game time, the temperature had dropped about 35 degrees. It was as if summer had turned to fall in a twinkling. Another bad omen.

Walking to the stadium for the final game, I found myself momentarily alone with Alex DeFazio. We had just finished the window-smashing practice session, and for some reason I was feeling pretty reflective.

"Well, Alex," I said. "You've been to the mountaintop. You made it all the way to Williamsport, Pennsylvania. The Little League World Series. You and your teammates are the champions of the entire United States. You have stories for your grandchildren. So, tell me, when you look back on it all, what is your most cherished memory?"

He didn't hesitate a second. "Breaking car windows and trying to pick up babes in San Bernardino."

In the Long Beach section of the stadium, a marvelous little pre-game event had taken place.

During the U.S. championship game, ESPN showed the ubiquitous troll dolls that had been our mascots. As moms had done at other games, they had inserted some of the dolls in the foul screen. (It surprised me that an organization that has rules about sunflower seeds never stopped the moms from desecrating the foul screen.)

Now, just a couple of hours before game time, a carton arrived from Kirkland, Washington. Sent by the company that manufactures the dolls, the Ace Novelty Company, the carton contained a large troll for each kid on the team. We were becoming famous from coast to coast.

Taylor John sang the national anthem and Vice President Dan Quayle threw out the first ball. (Steve and Donna Warshauer were back home for two weeks before discovering that Jeff still had the Dan Quayle ball.) Also taking part in the opening ceremonies were basketball legend Kareem Abdul-Jabbar, actor Tom Selleck, and syndicated columnist and author George Will.

Tommy John told me how, when he was with the Dodgers, Kareem now and then took batting practice with the team. According to John, he couldn't hit fastballs.

Earlier in the day, Denny Mayfield had been running somewhere on an errand when a limousine pulled up and deposited Selleck. Without breaking stride, Denny said, "Hey, Tom, baby. Glad you could make it."

While the ceremonies were unfolding, a little prayer was running through my mind. "Merciful God, please don't let our guys get killed here."

Cars had started arriving at 9 a.m., and by game time, the crowd estimate was 42,000, the largest crowd ever to see a Little League World Series. About half the fans were spread out, picnic blankets and all, across the hilly lawns overlooking the stadium. It was a stirring scene, the kind of thing you imagine when you think of the United States at its best.

Back in Long Beach, commerce had pretty much come to a standstill. Almost everyone was in front of a television set.

Down the coast, in Costa Mesa, Denny's brother, Travis, was getting married in a hotel. The groom arranged for a television to be set up beside the wedding party. Throughout the nuptials, he alternated between looking at his bride and looking at the TV.

When the knot was tied, the entire wedding party settled in and watched the rest of the game.

I had one thin hope. Old and big as the Filipinos were, I noticed they suffered from the usual Little League flaw: They could not hit a curveball. And Ryan Beaver, our starting pitcher (Sean was ineligible by virtue of having pitched in the national championship), had a pretty good curve on some days.

But, alas, Ryan was having a bad curveball day. Then, to compound things, bad luck simply set in. (After all the luck we had that summer, we were probably due.) The Filipino kids started hitting balls that would just stay within the foul lines or would fall into the gaps.

Since the Filipinos would almost stand on the plate, defying us to throw inside, there was also the small matter of Ryan hitting four batters in the head—all with curveballs, I should note.

What happened that afternoon showed how difficult it was for 11- and 12-year-olds to play baseball against kids who are older. By the bottom of the third, the boys (boys?) from Zamboanga were ahead, 8 to 0. Then a couple of our guys walked, and another got a single. Up stepped Ryan Stuart and hit a grand-slam home run to left field.

(For the next few weeks, when you telephoned the Stuart house, you got an answering-machine recording that said, "This is the home of Ryan Stuart, the boy who hit the grand-slam homer against those cheaters from the Philippines.")

Ryan, our first baseman, was another kid who made our team special. Earlier in the year, he had been diagnosed as having the Epstein-Barr virus, also known as chronic fatigue symdrome.

Holding his own with other kids was a struggle. But struggle he did, aided by weekly gamma globulin shots. When, for some reason, he could not get his shot during World Series week, his older brother, Chad, recharged him with B-12 via massive amounts of orange juice.

In addition, a year earlier, his family had realized

he was dyslexic. His brain saw words and letters different-ly from their actual order.

Ryan was bummed out by the discovery. Until one night when his mom, Peggy, called him into the living room to hear a TV interview with a man talking of prob-lems he had encountered as a dyslexic youngster. The man was pitcher Nolan Ryan of the Texas Rangers.

Said Peggy later, "Nolan Ryan will never know what he did for my son that day."

It was 8 to 4 now, and I began thinking, "Could this be pos-sible? After all, we've been the team of destiny all year long. Could we actually pull this game out?"

The answer was no. The Philippine manager was taking no chances. Having started with Ignacio Ramacho, who, believe it or not, was said to be their fifth-best pitch-er, they now brought in their third-best, Ian Tolentino.

The new guy looked like Roger Clemens. He was throwing about 75 miles per hour. Third best?

On our side, Ryan Beaver pitched his heart out. He never cried, never asked to be taken out. I really felt for the guy. When we did take him out and put in Randall Shelley, Ryan came into the dugout and said, "Coach, I don't be-lieve it. Everything I threw up there, they hit   balls in the dirt, balls over their heads. Everything."

The Filipinos were still bombing us at the bat, but I no-ticed an odd thing. They would swing at a pitch, miss it, and grin. Swing, miss, and grin. It was almost as if they were trying to strike out so as not to run up the score to 25 or 30 runs and make people suspicious. They were missing the ball. And laughing.

Late in the game, Jeff Warshauer started crying out of frustration. One of the wire services got a photo of him standing there in all his catcher's equipment with the tears coming down his cheeks. The picture ran in a lot of newspapers around the country. In a strange way, it was a lovely photo, showing how intense kids' baseball can get. Steve and Donna Warshauer treasure it.

Kids need to understand losing as well as winning. I tried to get them not to take the games as if they were life and death matters. Before some games, I would tell them, "There are a billion Chinese who don't gave a darn about this game."

That didn't seem to work with our guys. They would look at me strangely. Maybe they didn't get the point. Or maybe they couldn't figure out what the Chinese had to do with their games.

For all the horror that was taking place, our kids were having a surprisingly good time. (Sean, however, was still feeling pretty grim from the flu.)

Toward the end, we wanted all the guys to get in the game. We sent David Gonzalez in to bat for Ali. He struck out on four pitches and came back to the dugout. Ali said, "Why did they send you in? I could have struck out on my own." There was a big laugh over that. You would not have believed our guys were getting hammered.

The final score was 15 to 4. The Philippines team made the traditional run around the field carrying the world championship flag. For a town as small as Williamsport, it had a surprisingly sizeable Filipino community. So the team had a considerable cheering section on hand.

Angry as I felt, we were still truly happy for them. They may have been older, but they were still kids—and Third World kids at that. It was likely this was as good as some of their lives ever would get.

I shook hands with their manager, their coach, and with the kids. They all seemed kind of surprised by this. Maybe they don't do that sort of thing over there.

Our guys shed a few tears after the game, but not many. I gave a sort of farewell address to them and got pretty teary-eyed myself. We had come a long way together. For all their misbehavior, for all the headaches they had given Larry and me, I realized at the end that I had come to love each one of these little guys with all my heart.

We kind of broke up then. The adults went off to dinner, and the kids went off to...well, they went off to being kids again. A half hour or so after the game, they were running amok, stopping elevators and, in general, destroying a couple of Williamsport hotels.

About midnight, when we were back together in the barracks and asleep, there was a knock on the door. One of the uncles informed us that there would be a wake-up call at 2:30 a.m. They had booked us on a 7 a.m. flight out of Harrisburg.

It was ridiculous. We had just finished playing the World Series a few hours ago, and now they were anxious to get us out of there. Also, we had been looking forward to having a nice breakfast and taking a last look at the stadium.

But no. At 2:30 a.m., we climbed out of bed, packed —bats, balls and everything—and headed down the road to Harrisburg.

We were well on our way home by the time Sunday's *Sun-Gazette* began arriving on the porches of Williamsport homes.

In it, Creighton Hale, Little League's head man, declared that the World Series just completed had been "the very finest in the 50-year history of our organization."

Less than a month later, he would be scrambling to save face for his organization.

Unlike the trip east, this time there was no hideous layover in St. Louis to give the kids extra time to misbehave. Instead, there was a hideous layover in Atlanta.

On the spot, I gave up any claim I might have had to the title of team disciplinarian. Putting cotton in my ears, I fell asleep on the floor of the terminal. And let the kids do what they did best: misbehave.

On the plane going home, I thought of what the kids had accomplished. It was astonishing. They had won 22 consecutive games and scored 175 runs (while their opponents had scored 51). We had 53 home runs against 12 by opposing teams.

Our pitchers (Sean, Ryan Beaver, and Dane Mayfield) had pitched 134 innings for a combined ERA of 1.9%.

When we landed in Los Angeles that afternoon, the pilot announced that they would let the other passengers leave the plane first because there was a large group inside the terminal waiting to greet the Little League Champions of the United States.

Our kids did not know what he was talking about. They still hadn't quite caught on to what they had accomplished in winning the national championship.

After they won it, I had tried to prepare them for what was coming. "You have no idea what will happen over the next couple of months. You will remember it five, ten, thirty years from now." Still, they just weren't prepared for it.

They were still kids. My little babies, I kept calling them.

In the terminal, they walked out into a sea of several hundred people, including the media, the mayor of Long Beach, Ernie Kell, and a cadre of little girl groupies. (Alex loved it.)

They put us on a couple of buses and drove us to Stearns Park, our home field in Long Beach. The band from Wilson, my old high school, was there to greet us. I didn't know whether to cry or be ill. It happens that I have a stomach condition from way back when. For the first time in three or four years, it was back. A small price to pay, however, for a national championship.

It was about then that I remembered my car was 100 miles away—at the airport in Ontario. My stomach flipped again.

On Tuesday, we had the parade that had been organized by John Morris, the restaurateur, and the Downtown Long

Beach Association. The *Press-Telegram* put out a special souvenir section, and 20,000 people turned out along a five-block area of the city's Pine Avenue. There were open convertibles for the kids, and bands, and confetti fired from some sort of cannons mounted on the roofs of buildings.

The parade was followed by a ceremony in which the kids received proclamations from city officials, plus a variety of gifts, including sports shoes from one shoe manufacturer.

There were the inevitable speeches and introduction of politicians. It got a tad tedious, but during it all, anyone wanting comic relief could watch William Stuart. Throughout the ceremony, Ryan's dad sat in a chair facing the crowd of several thousand people—while a professional barber shaved off his beard for the first time in 20 years.

For the kids, that was the start, the beginning of a couple of months of community breakfasts, appearances, parades, and so on (including the Hollywood Christmas Parade). Sean had received an individual invitation to appear on a certain TV show. But because it conflicted with the day of the downtown parade and because he wanted to be with the team, he said no to David Letterman.

Much as I would have liked to see Sean on the David Letterman show myself, I was really proud of the decision he made.

Rightly or wrongly, almost everyone in the media wanted a crack at the kids. Talk shows called from all around the country, and we went on a few of them. We also went on "The Todd Donohoe Show," a sports TV program that, in Los Angeles, follows "Monday Night Football."

Todd called me a Bill Clinton look-alike. I'm not sure he was right about that, but it was a pretty nice feeling to be compared in any regard to the guy who was about to be elected president.

Things never really got back to normal, but in a couple of weeks they got...well, less hectic. School had started, which was probably a good thing for the kids. Once again, they were doing homework (in some cases) and going to soccer practice.

Larry went back to his law practice and apologized to everyone in the firm for his long absence. One of the guys looked him in the eye and said, "It isn't just all the time you missed from work. It's also all the time we missed from work while we were following the team. But the bottom line, you son of a gun, is that you lived my dream."

Needless to say, the guy is a Little League manager.

In the early evening of September 17, the phone rang at our house. One of our local league officials was asking us, along with the other team families, to gather immediately at Stearns Park.

Word had just come from Williamsport. For having illegal players, the team from the Philippines had been stripped of its title.

By default, we had been named the Little League champions of the world.

Part Two

fourteen

My wishful thinking for a crusading journalist had come true. His name was Al Mendoza, and he worked in, of all places, Manila, the capital of the Philippines.

On the day of the parade in Long Beach, Bob McKittrick, administrator of our Little League district, was phoned by an Associated Press reporter in Manila. "What did you think about the story in the *Philippine Inquirer?*" the guy asked.

Since McKittrick does not have Manila's two dozen newspapers delivered to his house in Long Beach, he had no idea what the AP man was talking about. The reference, however, was to a story—actually a column—written by Mendoza in the *Philippine Daily Inquirer*.

It had appeared that morning as Manila was showering its Little League champs with a ticker-tape parade. Starting with, "I hate to be a killjoy, but..." the story said birth certificates had been falsified to enable overage players to join the All-Stars.

Further, the alleged ages of players did not jibe with records at the National Bureau of Census and Statistics. At least eight of the 14 players were overage, Mendoza wrote, including Ian Torentino, one of the pitchers against us.

McKittrick said that, for the sake of the Philippine kids, he hoped the story was not true. But if it was true, he told the AP man, "then my kids are the champs. And I'm going to fight for my kids."

In Williamsport, the reaction was of less stern stuff. "We do not respond to newspaper articles or accusations from outside the Little League organizations," said spokesman Dennis Sullivan.

Little League, he added, had no intention of investigating the Philippine team. Unless someone filed a protest.

From the moment Mendoza's story appeared, Philippine officials rallied to the defense of their country's Little League team. So did most of the media. Brutal comments were hurled at Mendoza. He guessed, correctly, that they would get worse.

Mendoza realized people did not want to hear the truth about the team. The kids were heroes. On behalf of the government, President Fidel Ramos had presented the team with a gift of $41,166. The money was to be divided among the players for educational or living expenses.

At home, watching Manila's parade on TV, Mendoza tried to get drunk on beer. And couldn't.

Among those downplaying Mendoza's findings was Sergio Bernal, the country's top Little League official. "It is unfortunate that efforts are being mounted to discredit the hard-earned and well-deserved victory of the Philippine team that won the Little League Baseball World Series championship."

All the Zamboanga players had legal birth certificates, he insisted.

Another official expressed fear that the claims of cheating would overshadow the world championship. Winning it, he said, had been "as big a sports event that we'll have in a decade."

If Williamsport was not willing to take action on behalf of the U.S. team, McKittrick was. A district administrator who was not afraid to buck the Little League brass, he formed a makeshift task force to assemble proof that the Philippines had used illegal players. It included a Philippine senator, some media people, and a couple of U.S. State Department workers in Manila. Within days, his phone bill to the Philippines passed the $2,000 mark.

When he thinks back on all of it now, the thing that still rankles is the fact that Williamsport "never even called me. Not once."

Indeed, the capital of Little League seemed supremely indifferent to events unfolding in the capital of the Philippines. These included a press conference in which pitcher

Tolentino was asked his age. He said he was about to turn 13. But moments later, he admitted having played in a Bronco League tournament, in which players had to be at least 13. That had been two years ago.

There were two possibilities: 1. Someone had cheated by putting him on the Zamboanga team. 2. He was not aging at all, perhaps the first such case since Jack Benny turned 39.

On the condition of anonymity, a former Philippines Little League coach said such cheating was common in the country. Why? Because in the Far East, he said, "everybody else is doing it." In 1984, he claimed, Little League officials even removed body hair from overage Filipino players.

(It was later reported that hair removal in the Philippines was done with tweezers. The Dominican Republic approach was said to be less painful. They reportedly used Nair.)

Mendoza and his newspaper kept after the story despite unpleasant messages phoned to the *Inquirer* and Mendoza. "I hope you die soon," said one caller. As if to certify the first caller's wish, another phoned to say, "You're not going to live long."

At a Kentucky Fried Chicken, he was recognized by a woman, who said, "Mendoza, you're dirt." A couple of other people joined in and started berating him. In an editorial, a rival paper accused him of having a "crab mentality."

For all the complaints about Mendoza, however, there was growing evidence that the world champions had cheated.

Or, more precisely, that the adults responsible for the team had cheated.

Eduardo Toribio, original manager of the Zamboanga team, said eight local boys had been bounced to make room for players from other parts of the Philippines. While our All-Star team had been selected from, essentially, one neighborhood in Long Beach, it was being suggested that the Philippines' All-Star team had been chosen from a pool of 67 million people.

What's more, ex-manager Toribio said he had been pushed aside himself in favor of Rodolfo Lugay, a former player who was director of the Rizal Memorial Baseball Stadium in Manila and was known as the "Babe Ruth of the Philippines."

McKittrick's allies in the Philippines assembled clippings from newspapers that had covered the country's national Little League tournament. They showed that some players who went to Williamsport had played for teams other than Zamboanga. Tolentino, for example, had been the losing pitcher for Cavite in a game against Zamboanga.

Relations between the United States and the Philippines were already strained, in part over the closing of U.S. military facilities there. Now what had seemed to some a relatively minor Little League scandal threatened to mushroom into a diplomatic schism.

In Los Angeles, the consul general of the Philippines called a news conference and further muddied the waters by admitting that overage players were used. But he said it was a conspiracy by a group wishing to embarrass youth baseball in the Philippines.

He did not name this group. Nor did he give a reason as to why it wanted to "discredit our boys."

By now, even Williamsport had been moved to action. Hale, president and chief executive officer of Little League Baseball, faxed a query to Armando Andayo, a district administrator in the Philippines.

Andayo caved in. Yes, eight players from outside the district had been put on the team illegally. The changes were made, he said, after Zamboanga won the national championship. And, yes, again, he also said he had been involved in similar cheating for the past five years.

In Long Beach, league officials planned to meet September 18 to draft a formal protest to Williamsport. The meeting never took place. Late on the 17th, we got word: Williamsport had taken the world title from the Philippines. We were the champs.

By phone network, players and parents were summoned to Stearns Park for a victory celebration. The media, including TV stations from Los Angeles, were out in full force. But it was a hollow victory party, as reflected by statements the kids gave to the press.

"I guess we won," said Ali Strain-Bay.

Kevin Miller (without resorting to a single expletive) said, "It stinks that the Philippines would cheat like that, but I'd feel a lot better if we had won the game."

"I'm sorry we didn't play the game and had to have it handed down," Jeff Warshauer added.

Randall Shelley expressed what a lot of us were feeling. "I think we should play them again," he said.

Sean stayed home to watch "The Simpsons."

In the Philippines, Andayo resigned from Little League. He accused the United States and Little League of sour grapes.

"The Americans in Williamsport just could not take it at the hands of the Filipinos," he said. "Hence, they scrounged around for some reason to overturn the victory."

For a time, Andayo and others talked of suing Little League officials in Williamsport and Long Beach. But some time later, the Philippine senate issued a report. Among other things, it proposed sanctions, even criminal prosecution, for adults reponsible for the scandal.

After that, we heard nothing more about a lawsuit.

Ironically, the reason Williamsport used in dethroning the team was the failure of some players to meet the residency requirement. Technically, they never did deal with the age issue.

In the Philippines, newspapers that had gone after Mendoza now turned on the United States.

"U.S. officials...stripped our little boys of the title without asking for our side of the controversy," the *Philippine Daily Globe* editorialized on its front page.

"It's pathetic the way we continue to be treated abroad for the simple reason that we are too patient and polite," said Max Soliven, publisher of the *Philippine Star*. "In the case of the Little League double-cross, let's raise a howl."

The *Daily Malaya* suggested the U.S., having failed to win the Vietnam War, had now "proclaimed themselves ...press release winners."

Geez, guys, it was only a baseball game.

But in Zamboanga, the editor of the *Daily Star*, Felino Santos, put the blame squarely on Little League officials in Manila. "It's about time that the people in this area say, 'You people in Manila have gone too far. You people in Manila are riding roughshod over us.'"

"The whole baseball system in the Philippines should be condemned. And the winning team of Zamboanga has been robbed of sending all its boys, who have been training for months. If this had not been manipulated in Manila, we could have sent our entire team."

Later, Little League in Williamsport did some backpedaling. Steve Keener, first vice president, claimed they had been suspicious of the Philippine team from the start. The manager and coach "didn't seem typical," he said.

Really? Then why had Creighton Hale called the 1992 Little League World Series "the very finest" ever?

In October, Mendoza, who writes on a variety of sports subjects, went to Canada to receive a golf-writing award. From there, he flew to Southern California to visit a sister. By phone, he arranged to have dinner with McKittrick and finally meet the voice at the other end of all those trans-Pacific phone conversations.

Meaning well, McKittrick and others planned a surprise. Instead of a quiet dinner, they brought him to Ciravello's, pizza headquarters of the Long Beach All-Stars, and made him a guest of honor at a dinner for the new world champs. Alas for Mendoza, the gesture backfired.

The slight Mendoza—he is 5-foot-6 and weighs only 135 pounds—was given a key to the city, a plaque, and a Long Beach All-Stars baseball cap. The man truly had no idea any of this was going to happen.

To please his hosts, he put the cap on and smiled for a photographer.

Two days later, the photo appeared in newspapers in Manila. Just when it seemed to be dying down, the crucifixion of Al Mendoza began anew.

"The name of Al Mendoza will live in infamy among his fellow Filipinos," said a writer for the *Manila Standard*. In other papers, Mendoza was—take your pick—a Judas Iscariot, a Vidkun Quisling, a Tokyo Rose.

Standing behind Mendoza, the *Inquirer* dug up new facts that confirmed the cheating. Although other reporters uncovered this data, Mendoza continued to take the heat.

An editorial in the rival *Manila Chronicle* read: "As to Mr. Al Mendoza, let us be reminded that rats have gone down in history with ignominious epitaphs, most of them well deserved. Al Capone had a way of disposing of rats. He bashed their heads with a baseball bat."

Mendoza responded by showing a flair for melodrama, writing, "If truth shall prevail, for truth had always been my beacon, then to hell with death."

Still, between home and office, he now had a bodyguard.

McKittrick and his assistant administrator, Ron Nelson, wrote to President Ramos. "We wish the people of the

Philippines to understand we do not blame them or any of the children," it said. "On the contrary, we know, because of Al Mendoza, that the people of the Philippines are a wonderful and honorable people."

Proposing that a Little League "sister program" be established between Long Beach and Zamboanga, they tried to get Mendoza off the hook for his having attended the dinner in Long Beach.

"Unknown to him, our mayor presented him with the key to our city, not for helping Long Beach Little League, but for being a man of integrity, honesty, and courage. All of your countrymen should be proud of this man."

Their letter was never answered.

Three months after his first column on the scandal, Al Mendoza was still being called a "traitor" on the streets of Manila.

In November, Mendoza's paper, the *Daily Inquirer*, ran a six-part series on the cheating scandal. It raised the possibility that not a single player on the team had been legal, and it said that even parents and teachers had taken part in the fraud.

The newspaper uncovered several cases of players who used two names.

Late in the year, *Sports Illustrated* sent writer Richard Hoffer to the Philippines. Journeying all the way to Zamboanga, 540 miles from Manila (the final leg on a ferry that transports oxen), he found a jungle city of 500,000, where people swapped stories of smuggling, plus the tale of a Japanese soldier said to have wandered out of the vegetation two years earlier to ask who had won the Second World War.

Hoffer's report, "Field of Schemes," described a scandal without end. One layer would be peeled away only to reveal another. By the time of his visit, boys whose names and birth certificates had been used were demanding financial tribute from boys who had gone to Williamsport.

Hoffer told how Armand Nocum, Zamboanga correspondent for the *Daily Inquirer*, disputed Mendoza's findings and set out to defend the team and the honor of his city. But his investigation only confirmed Mendoza's reports. The Zamboangan correspondent was enraged.

"The corruption in this country stinks," he said. "It's everywhere. But for God's sake, can we not spare the children?"

Back when it seemed that the Philippine players were the world champs, a congresswoman from the country, a member of a wealthy plantation family, had given a cash gift to the players.

One, who may or may not have been the team's shortstop, took his share and bought a cow to help provide for his family.

It was all terribly sad.

And perhaps saddest of all was the absolute conviciton I and others had that if Al Mendoza had not blown the whistle on the people in his own country, the cheating would have gone on forever.

fifteen

BRADY WERNER

Height: 5'6"
Weight: 130

Hit 10 home runs and compiled a
.351 average in tournament play.
Brady got a key hit to keep the
team alive in the Southern
California divisionals. He became a
household name in Long Beach for
his gritty and victorious pitching
during the internationally televised
world championship game against
Panama.

A few days before Christmas, our young world champions joined other world champions, the Toronto Blue Jays, to meet President George Bush at the White House. The team moms went along, as did Larry Lewis and Tony De-Fazio.

The Blue Jays graciously hosted a party for our kids. Then, after meeting the President the next morning, there was a White House tour. It was exciting, but not nearly as exciting as the trip Larry arranged that afternoon for the kids to meet the Washington Redskins.

On the unfamiliar Washington subway system, it took them an hour to get to RFK Stadium. Larry's contact with the Redskins had neglected to mention, however, that the team was not at RFK Stadium. It was practicing 60 miles away in Virginia. My wife panicked. What to do now?

"No problem," said Larry.

There was a expressway nearby. Larry the Legend ran to it, and began flagging cars, buses, UPS trucks—anyone. Finally, he hailed a guy driving a derelict station wagon taxicab that reeked of marijuana.

The driver, a Jamaican, did not want to go to Virginia. He especially did not want to go to Virginia with 13 kids and Larry in his cab.

"No problem," said Larry. "I'll give you $50."

"He'll give you $100," said the generous Dane Mayfield. "Stop bidding against me, Dane," whispered Larry.

The guy agreed to take them to Virginia. For $275. The kids and Larry piled into the cab. With reggae music blaring, it took off, went one block, and blew all four tires.

"I need new tires, mon," said the driver.

"No problem," said Larry.

The ride cost Larry $275 and a set of tires, and resulted in their arriving 3½ hours late to meet the Redskins. On the other hand, they had a great time.

A new year began, and the Little League calendar came around full circle. We had try-outs again, followed by the draft.

As manager and coach of the world championship team, other adults in the Long Beach league now seemed to give us a bit more respect. But not much more.

There were, in fact, two schools of thought regarding Larry and me. One held, rather grudgingly, that apparently we did know what we were doing. The other held that the players were so good, they could have won under the direction of Cheech and Chong.

Memories still burned over last year's scandal and the apparent years of cheating in Williamsport, which Long Beachers now regarded, rightly or wrongly, as the most despicable place in America outside of Congress.

Several parents had written to Little League in Williamsport. One, Steve Warshauer, accused Williamsport of winking at the cheating for years. He got a testy reply from Little League's boss, Creighton Hale. It said, in part:

"For your information, the decision [to dethrone the Philippines] was made following a thorough investigation by the Tournament Committee. There had been many unfounded allegations in the media, which is not uncommon following any championship game in which a team from the United States is defeated."

The toughest letter to Hale was probably from Dawn Shelley, the team mom who had cowed the uncles in last year's ticket episode.

"When we got to Williamsport, we were stunned to see a team so obviously overage as the Dominicans so shamelessly playing a boys' game...At the barbecue after the national championship game, I personally caught three Dominican players 'making out' in the shadows of the barracks with local shameless Williamsport girls. And I mean heavy petting. This was not the behavior of 11- and 12-year-old boys."

Dawn proposed several Little League reforms, then suggested the 1992 players be brought back to Williamsport, at Little League's expense, for the traditional victory run around the stadium and other world championship honors that had been denied them last year.

Predictably, that did not happen.

On the positive side, league president Bill Marshall could boast that Stearns Park had a new "snack shack," the concession stand that is a financial mainstay of Little League. In addition to the concession stand, the building included a league office and an announcer's booth.

It was the house the 1992 All-Stars built. In appreciation for those world championship thrills, people offered volunteer time, expert work, and donations. The building went up for about $40,000.

The structure included a trophy case designed and built by John Beaver. He spent a huge amount on this showcase for the world championship team, and he invited parents to provide museum-type items for display. The response was minimal, and by opening day, when the trophy case was to be unveiled, there was still a lot of empty space.

Hastily, John put in a few items to be replaced as other items came in from parents. He included Ryan's cap, plus the home-run ball his son had hit to win the U.S. title game. There were framed newspaper photos of Sean in a victory pose after the U.S. title game and Ryan hitting the homer that won it.

John asked me to look at the case. I thought it was terrific.

But others did not. Parents screamed. One called it the "Ryan Beaver shrine." Some said the case should not include photos of an individual person and called for the immediate removal of shots of Sean and Ryan.

True, it had been a team effort. John had even put a team photo in the case. But some parents acted like jerks, as if he had never solicited mementoes of their kids. Also, people did not understand that some of the items were temporary. John was crestfallen.

The league removed items, including the photos of Sean and Ryan. It was like Stalin being de-emphasized in the old Soviet Union. They put in pictures of each kid and nearly drove themselves crazy trying to be sure each picture was "equal" to the other pictures.

Some parents complained to me about the trophy case. I told them they should have built it themselves.

The trophy case brouhaha showed that, post-Williamsport, the unity of the parents had broken down. There were meetings now and then to discuss situations that came up, but there had been no such meeting over the trophy case. Things had gotten out of whack—and silly. No one could tell me the case should not include a picture of Ryan hitting the U.S. championship home run. We had come a long way from the magic moments of Williamsport.

Our regular-season team, the Pirates, continued to be disliked by the other teams, mostly because we were going after our fourth consecutive league title.

Everyone does *not* always love a winner, despite what you have heard to the contrary.

In point of fact, the Pirates did win the title again, which meant that once more Larry and I would pilot the All-Star team. After last year's experience, becoming a member of the All-Star team became a measure of status—not so much for the kids, but for the parents.

Word went around that one woman was willing to have sex with Larry to get her son on the 1993 team. It was a joke, of course. But her husband mused, "Well, if that's what it takes..."

Names of players chosen for the All-Star team are announced at the annual ceremony closing the league's regular season. It is a great day for those selected, and, of course, a tough day for the kids who are not. My wife, Deborah, thinks of it as the day that enables us to cut our Christmas card list in half.

One kid who did not make the 1993 team (and probably should have) was from a family that was very close to me. He was extremely distraught, and I tried to explain that there were only 14 slots on the team and that we just couldn't work him into one. He said he never wanted to talk to me again.

There were times when I wondered why I did this.

The method of choosing All-Stars varies from league to league. In ours, as mentioned earlier, the league's players vote for 12 members of the team and the manager and coach choose the other two.

It is a simple enough procedure, but parents of kids who are not chosen sometimes just refuse to believe that's the way it works. They think all the kids are chosen by the manager and coach. The result is a recurring conversation that goes like this:

Parent: "Larry, I think Fauntleroy should have been picked for the All-Star team. He had a better year than Makepeace, who was picked."

Larry: "Your son, Fauntleroy, had a great year. Personally, I also thought he should have been on the team. But the kids picked the players, not us. And they picked Makepeace."

Fauntleroy's pop would mull that over a few days, then, next time he saw Larry, would say:

"Larry, I think Fauntleroy should have been picked for the..."

It's as if the first conversation had never taken place. A couple of weeks would go by, and one day at the ballpark you would overhear the dad in question telling a friend, "You know, Larry and Jeff don't like Fauntleroy..."

One father confronted Larry with a computer print-out that, he said, proved his son, X, was better than another kid, Y. Both kids had grown up together, were good friends and exceptional athletes, but X's father was treating it as if Y, if named an All-Star, would go on to become the president of the United States.

Y, in fact, was named. The fathers of X and Y have not spoken to each other since. The kids are still good friends.

As we got into All-Star play, we tried not to think about our chances of returning to Williamsport. That was almost impossible. Attendance had been up at regular season games, and now people were speculating on whether this year's team was better than last year's All-Star Club.

One big factor in our favor was the return of four players from the 1992 team. (That reflected the wisdom of our drafting nine-year-olds way back when.)

Alex DeFazio was back, an inch taller, but still about the size of a loaf of bread. The Miller twins were back, and Kevin's vocabulary of expletives seemed even larger than last year's.

Sean, too, was back, and he was a much stronger edition than the 1992 Sean. At age 12, his wrists already were about the size of mine, and he was cultivating a fast-ball that could intimidate a major-leaguer. Well, okay, a bad major-leaguer.

Having Alex back also meant the return of his parents, Tony and Candy, probably the most nervous parents in the history of Little League. Watching them in the stands during a game was exhausting.

Tony, a foreman in a glass factory and a former national handball champion, is one of those guys who lives or dies with every pitch and cannot stay seated. Candy, whom I have known since high school, would be a basket case if Alex were pitching and had a 200-run lead.

We had 10 new kids on the block. One was a big, shy kid named Brady Werner, who had a queasy stomach. Before a game, his tummy would turn into a washing machine. I'd ask him if he could play, and he'd say, "I don't feel real good, Coach. But I will play. I can't let the team down."

I loved the kid.

As Brady's performance improved on the field, his stomach improved as well. Still, just before one of our big games, he looked at me, and said, "Coach, I've never played in front of so many people before. I've got some butterflies."

I thought it was really cute of him to admit that. But that is one of the charming things about kids this age: They wear their hearts on their sleeves.

Our local paper, the *Press-Telegram*, seemed determined to generate All-Star fever—if not All-Star hysteria.

Don't get me wrong. The paper had been good to us, and it supported our team as I suspect no other paper would support a Little League team. But now they began to use, on page one, a logo that read, "THE ROAD TO WILLIAMSPORT." They even ran a pull-out section with biographies of the kids. All this before we even played a game.

I worried that things such as that would put too much pressure on the kids. After all, they were not the Dallas Cowboys. In fact, they were not even the team that had made it to Williamsport last year. Ten of the 14 players were brand new. And because they were brand new, virtually an entirely different team, the odds against Long Beach going to Williamsport again were astronomical.

The newspaper, however, almost treated it as if a repeat were certain.

That publicity frenzy, plus our performance last year, had an effect. Our first All-Star game in 1992 had been played before about 150 people, most of them the families of players. Our first All-Star game in 1993 drew a crowd of about 4,000. They stood three and four deep beyond the outfield fence. There were announcers, TV cameras, and reporters from the *Press-Telegram, Orange County Register* and *Los Angeles Times.*

They saw Sean pitch a no-hitter against a team from the nearby Plaza League. We won the game, 13 to 0.

Next came the All-Stars from the town of Bellflower, and we beat them, 11 to 0.

Our third game, however, was scary. In a couple of ways.

Because of his heart condition and the pig valve inserted years ago, Larry tried to stay calm under the most trying circumstances. And our game against a neighboring league, Lakewood-Cerritos, was pretty trying. A scoreless tie, in fact, going into the fourth inning.

Larry got up from the bench intending to put a substitute player into the game. He was walking toward the umpire when he began to weave and wound up leaning against a fence.

Time was called. A doctor came onto the field. In a matter of minutes, Larry was feeling better and had been pronounced fit by the doctor.

As the game resumed, I said, "It will probably take a close game like this to kill you instead of one of those tense courtroom battles you go through."

"Probably," he conceded. "But Little League baseball is much more important than anything that goes on in a courtroom."

Oh, yes, we won the game. 11 to 0.

Next, we beat the Los Altos All-Stars, 11 to 4, and again, 7 to 0, for the district title. Now there were three tournaments between us and Williamsport. We tried hard not to think of Pennsylvania. But that was not easy. The *Press-Telegram* kept up the hype, and I began to see the "Road to Williamsport" logo in my dreams.

Brady Werner hit a grand-slam homer in that last game. In so doing, however, he showed there is no end to the problems of a Little Leaguer. "I felt real happy rounding the bases," he said later, "but I didn't know if I should smile too much or not. So I tried to control it."

You won't find stuff like that in *The Baseball Encyclopedia*.

sixteen

BILLY GWINN

Height: 5′3″
Weight: 105

Every great ballplayer seems to have a secret source of strength. Billy claims to get his from his beagle puppy, Samantha. As a catcher, he performed the amazing feat of not allowing a single passed ball during the entire all-star season. He was an inspiration to his teammates and an example of hard, unselfish work.

The performance of last year's All-Stars inspired one Little Leaguer to try to become a member of the 1993 team. His name was Cassidy Traub.

     Small and only 11 years old, he was not a good All-Star prospect. But I don't think I ever saw a kid so determined to make a team. From fall to spring, he visited the batting cages four times a week. That's an enormous commitment for an 11-year-old. It paid off. He made the team.

Charlie Hayes was also 11, but different in other respects. That became evident one afternoon later in the season when the kids, in the throes of clowning around, suddenly stopped to stare in wonder at Charlie, who was doing a very strange thing.

He was reading a book.

The team was dumbfounded. It was as if he had been caught in an un-macho act, such as talking to a girl. "Charleeee is rrrrreading!" (I think the book was *The Firm*, by John Grisham.)

In danger of becoming an outcast, he promised his teammates he would never read again.

We had three 11-year-olds, the third being our catcher, Billy Gwinn. The kids at one point were asked by a newspaper to list their most important wishes. Billy's was "to go to heaven with everyone in my family on the same day."

It was touching to see how much little boy still resided inside most of these kids.

We moved up to the next level, the Section Tournament. We won it in three games, scoring a total of 30 runs against 1 by our opponents.

The third game of the tournament was a tense and somewhat astonishing episode that took only one hour and four minutes to play. Sean struck out 16. But the opposing team, Puente Hills, had a top-notch pitcher, Enoch Choi. Sean got to him in the third with a homer to left field.

Another 1 to 0 victory. Things were proving to be a tad tougher the second time around.

One of the new guys on the 1993 team was Larry's son, Timmy. He was letting his hair grow that summer, claiming that, like Samson, his strength came from his hair. Since he was a pretty good long-ball hitter, and Larry and I were taking no chances, he got away with not getting a haircut. By September, he looked like Prince Valiant.

(Billy Gwinn, by contrast, claimed to get his strength from his beagle puppy, Samantha. This wasn't exactly blood-and-guts baseball we were playing.)

Although he was the son of Larry the Legend, Timmy—dare I say it?—was not sure he wanted to be on the All-Star team. A surfer, he told his father, "Last year those guys missed the whole summer. Besides, you can't surf if you're on the All-Star team."

"Sure you can," Larry said. "You can surf between games."

"There's no surf in San Bernardino, Dad."

Larry silently cursed the school system for teaching too much geography. But, surfing or no, Timmy stayed on the team.

After wooing girls, Alex DeFazio's favorite pastime is browbeating promises from adults. Specifically, he developed a form of blackmail in which he would say, "Hey, if we win this game, can we do such and such?"

In most cases, Larry and I would agree, being essentially prepared to auction our souls for the cause of victory.

At one division tournament game at San Diego, Alex came up with, "Hey, Larry, if we win, can we drive your car?"

What's a manager to do? "Sure," said Larry. "You can drive my car."

That night, with Larry supervising in the passenger seat, Alex and a couple of other kids drove the Legend's Jaguar around the dirt parking lot of the Hickman Youth Sports Complex. Barely able to see over the steering wheel,

Alex whipped around in ever-tightening circles at high speeds.

(Later, the mechanic who performed the autopsy attributed the Jaguar's premature demise to this impromptu San Diego Driving Derby.)

As the dirt flew, the San Diego tournament director happened upon the scene, and he was outraged to think a manager would do such a thing.

I tried to smooth things over. Having been in cars in which Larry was driving, I tried to assure the guy that the situation might have been much worse had Larry been driving instead of one of the kids. He was not amused.

We won our first division tournament game against a San Diego team called Santana. It was a big day for one of our kids, Jeremy Hess.

Jeremy is a little guy—"about the size of Winnie the Pooh," said one of the newspaper writers. The nickname stuck, at least with Jeremy's family. Jeremy had not been hitting well up to that point. Before the game, Al Huntley took him aside, and, among other things, changed the boy's batting stance a bit.

Jeremy hit two homers that day, surprising everyone in the ballpark, including himself. One was a grand slam. The other drove in three runs. The game against Santana was a laugher. We won, 13 to 2.

Our next game, against Thousand Oaks, was a different kind of laugher. The final score was 16 to 1. For the first time in two seasons of All-Star play, we lost a game.

Al Miller, a commodities trader and the father of the twins, may be the most easygoing parent in the world. His only complaint about the team was a strange one. Or so it seemed at the time.

His complaint was that the team did not lose enough.

Al thought kids should understand losing as well as winning. It is a good philosophy, and I wish the world had more Al Millers.

In truth, we had tried to prepare the team for the possibility of losing a game. We had tried to instill in them a sense that it was not the worst thing that could happen.

Excluding the illegal game against the Philippines, we had compiled a consecutive victory string of 31 games before losing to Thousand Oaks. Our '93 All-Stars had gone into that game with a total of 87 runs against only 7 by our opponents.

So, what had gone wrong? Everything.

Larry explained it this way to Pamela Lewis, who covered the team for the *Press-Telegram*: "Everything that could go wrong for us did. And everything that could go right for them did. We were used to being on the other side. We know how it feels now to lose."

Even the Thousand Oaks coach, Sam East, was surprised by his team's lopsided victory. "No way did we think we would win the game like that," he said.

Kevin Miller, for one, was philosophical about the loss. "All we have to do now," he said, "is go undefeated."

He was right. The tournament was double elimination, meaning that one more loss would send us home. Now, to win the tournament and go to San Bernardino for the western regional, we would have to win five consecutive games. In five days.

Those games included a rematch against Thousand Oaks.

Said Larry, "We're going to be tested. We're going to see what kind of heart and soul this team has."

Alex DeFazio had pitched the game we lost to Thousand Oaks. "He felt terrible," recalls Tony, his father, "just devastated." It was one of those Little League situations that can result in a kid swearing off baseball forever.

But Tony handled it well. "Listen to me, Alex," he said. "It's not all your loss, not by any means. It was a loss by the team. There were a lot of errors in that game."

Our first game after the loss came the next day when we played South Mission Viejo. Sean gave up a home run in the first. By the fifth inning, we were still behind, 1 to 0, and I began thinking about a fishing trip to Mexico.

But Brady Werner hit a double that scored two runs, and we won another squeaker, 2 to 1. We needed four more wins.

Because teams in the losers' bracket have to play every day, we had to expand our pitching rotation.

We put Brady on the mound against West Covina, and for five innings he held them to three hits. But in the sixth, he gave up four hits, and it was a struggle for us to get that third out and win, 4 to 2. Three games to go.

On August 6, we played Thousand Oaks, the team that had clobbered us. In that game, they had gotten 13 hits.

This time, however, they got only two. Sean pitched, striking out the last five batters. Timmy Lewis homered. We won, 5 to 1. Now we only had to win two more.

Thousand Oaks had an outfielder who looked as if he had escaped from juvenile detention, the kind of guy who seemed ready to kill anyone who looked at him.

At the end of each game, it is traditional for players of both teams to line up and shake hands. But this kid apparently misunderstood the tradition. Instead of shaking hands, he punched each opposing player in the stomach. None of our kids would strike back because the guy was so fearsome.

I went to their coach and asked them to stop the kid. The coach said, "We've tried, but he punches us in the stomach, too."

It was around this time, I think, when Sandi Lewis told Larry one day, "You love Little League more than you love me."

"Maybe so," he said, "but I love you more than football and golf."

Alex DeFazio was back on the mound against Woodland Hills, and I wondered if he could bounce back from the 16-1 Thousand Oaks rocky horror show. He did. His curve broke well, his fastball was great, and the team seemed to be getting back its stride. Sean and Timmy Lewis hit two homers each, Brady hit one, and we triumphed, 13 to 4.

We needed one more victory to return to San Bernardino.

The double elimination tournament worked out in such a way that the final game was another match against Woodland Hills. It was no contest. We won, 14 to 5, and we seemed to have found ourselves again.

"I think the game we lost served as a wake-up call," Sean told sportswriter Pamela Lewis.

It was time to break out the camels, the canteens, and the rest of the desert gear. Once again, as Southern California's champions, we were headed for the western region tournament in San Bernardino.

The Northern California champion, for an unprecedented third consecutive time, was San Ramon Valley.

The grown-ups were celebrating our division championship with a party in Long Beach. I was ripping up the I-405 to get to it when my car engine quit.

The result was my first brush with legalized crime: specifically, a tow truck operator who charged me double. It was Sunday, and not easy to get a tow truck. When I protested, he said, "Take it or leave it."

I had him deposit the car in front of the bar where the party was in progress. When it comes to a party, I will not be denied.

seventeen

TIMMY LEWIS

Height: 5'6"
Weight: 127

"The Tim-inator" batted a torrid .460 during tournament play and helped the team win the Southern California division with home runs in three consecutive games. He also hit one of the longest homers ever seen in the Western Regional tournament. Timmy played left field, and he made a spectacular catch to save a no-hitter for Sean Burroughs.

As is bound to happen when things are going well, we had a sad experience. It involved the parents of one of our players, and I really let it get to me.

Perhaps I'm being oversensitive. I wanted everyone to like me and to like what Larry and I and the team were doing. But with 14 players and only nine baseball positions, that simply was not going to happen.

There was a movie years ago about an opera singer who wound up killing himself because he could not please one critic. Other critics loved him, but instead of basking in their praise, he let the negative guy destroy him. That's an extreme comparison, but I'm a little like that.

So is this little anecdote. We had 13 pairs of parents who were experiencing the time of their lives. But we had one pair I will call The Parents Grim.

They asked one day why their son—let's call him Throckmorton Grim—was not on the starting team.

"Right now," said Larry, "there are some other kids who are playing better than Throckmorton. But Throckmorton is a fine player, and his being on the All-Star team is proof of that. Moreover, we like Throckmorton very much."

The Parents Grim did not buy any of that. They had it in their heads that Larry and I did not like Throckmorton, and they were not going to be talked out of it. They tried to generate sympathy from the other parents. When that was not successful, they began sitting by themselves at games.

To this day, The Parents Grim have not talked to Larry or me.

On one occasion, later in the year, we were having a fundraiser in which each player donated an item to be auctioned off. Throckmorton's donation—inspired, I'm sure, by his parents—was apparently supposed to be symbolic of his having sat on the bench so much. (In truth, there were other boys who played even less.)

It was a handful of splinters.

At Larry's law firm, someone took the nameplate off the door to his office, and replaced it with another.

The new one read: Larry the Legend.

Two things made San Bernardino different this year.

One was the absence of our old antagonist, Chickie Walsh, who had stepped down—or, in his case, perhaps stepped up—from managing the San Ramon Valley team.

The other was a newly-installed air-conditioning system that really worked. Perhaps noticing that last year's tournament temperatures had gone as high as 118 degrees, the moguls of San Bernardino had roared into the 20th century by acquiring modern air-conditioning.

It was hard to know which pleased me more. The presence of the air-conditioning or the absence of Chickie.

We shared a barracks with the Montana team, as we had last year.

With a solid wall separating the teams, it was clear the barracks had been built with noise abatement in mind. Nevertheless, we heard the Montana boys on occasion. In turn, they apparently heard us every waking moment. Their coach rushed to our door one night and screamed at our guys to hold the noise down.

Frankly, I didn't think our kids had been that loud. But maybe I was getting used to them. Or maybe there is no such thing as hideous, ear-piercing, brain-jarring noise in Montana.

The first event of the tournament, once again, was the chief umpire's meeting with the managers and coaches. Instead of the long-winded Sy, the chief umpire this time was another long-winded guy who must have taken charm lessons from his predecessor.

He recited a billion or so rules, each of which seemed designed to get somebody thrown out of a game. Who says Little League has to be fun?

Our first tournament game was against Arizona, and we won, 13 to 4. Sean started, but our bats were so hot we pulled him after the first inning, thus leaving him eligible, according to Little League rules, to start the next game.

That was against the Spring Valley Little League of Las Vegas, Nevada. The team had a fine pitcher, Brian Bryant, who struck out 12 of our guys and held us to four hits.

Fortunately, his fastball was too fast for his own catchers (they used two), and there were nine passed balls. We won, 3 to 0, with Sean throwing a one-hitter.

Between games, as we had done last year with John Beaver, Larry and I pleaded for parent volunteers to spend a night supervising the kids in the barracks. This enabled us to slip away to the hotel, which, although not the crown jewel of the Hilton chain, was a veritable pleasure palace compared to the compound.

Asking a parent to take over in the barracks was comparable to asking a soldier to go over the top and lob a few grenades at the enemy while the rest of the regiment hunkers down in the trenches.

Not surprisingly, our efforts to recruit barracks honchos were not always successful. I asked Jim Werner, Brady's father, one afternoon, and he responded by laughing as loudly as it is possible for a human to laugh.

He would do anything for the team. He would help at practice. He would carry equipment. He would, if necessary, drive a truck of dynamite down a mountain road.

But spend a night in the barracks with the kids— or, as he preferred to call them, "those maniacs"? No way.

I explained that other parents had volunteered, but Jim had a ready rebuttal to that. He said the other parents must be stupid.

As Jim walked off, he was still laughing and muttering something about "never in a million years."

A team manager during the regular season, Jim, a gardener, did help out enormously in practice sessions. During one of them, he took a painful shot in the ribs by a line drive. Some day, I plan to do a study on what it would cost to insure a Little League father.

Larry managed to slip away for a few hours to attend to matters at his law firm. The backlog of work was enormous. A pile of messages awaited him, plus a pile of questions from his fellow barristers. The first of these was: Why did you pull Sean in the first inning of the game against Nevada?

More baseball questions followed, and it took Larry 45 minutes to reach his desk. When he did, the first person he saw was lawyer Catherine Page, who is veddy, veddy British. She gave her analysis of the last game.

"I think Timmy played very sensibly."

As was the case last year, pin-trading, even more than baseball, seemed the dominant interest of the players.

With some pins being worth much more than others and with the emphasis placed on out-trading the other guy, this seemingly innocent hobby can sometimes have a pretty dark side.

Just how dark was demonstrated by the mini-scandal we came to call "Pingate." It involved adults cheating kids.

What happened was this. Back in March, our older boy, Scott, an avid trader, had designed his own pin along with his friend Tom Sawdei, and he earned money at odd jobs so he could pay to have the pin manufactured in three colors. Deliberately, he arranged to have only a small number made. Doing this would increase their value when it came to trading.

His plan was to take the new pins to the San Bernardino tournament (whether or not the team got there) and spend most of his time in the large tent that serves as pin-trading headquarters during the games.

But adults got Scott and Tom's design and ordered up some pins on their own. They, too, counted on trading the pins at San Bernardino—probably never dreaming that Scott and Tom would be there or that the team would make a repeat appearance in the western tournament.

Eventually, it all blew over. There was one aspect to the whole thing, however, that was really unsettling.

The two adults were officials in our league.

Oh, yes, one of them did apologize.

eighteen

NATE MOEINY

Height: 4′10″
Weight: 95

Nate compiled a .303 batting average, and he hustled as much as anyone on the field. An outstanding runner, he would gallop through a brick wall if it would help the team. Nate played the outfield and contributed some great catches. He may be the only Little Leaguer in America whose favorite food is sushi.

For the ceremonies prior to our opening game, the tournament director chose the Miller twins to recite the Little League pledge. I had a gut feeling that would be a mistake.

It was. In front of 10,000 people, Chris and Kevin got a few words into the pledge and started to titter. The titters turned to giggles and the giggles turned to belly laughs. I was embarrassed for them. And more embarrassed for us.

Tiny as it may have been, the incident with the Miller twins was symbolic of the fact that things seemed less carefree this time around. Maybe it was because some of the mystery was gone. And maybe it was because we felt pressure to repeat last year's performance.

Whatever the case, nerves seem to be more frayed. In one game, Chris Miller struck out. As he returned to the dugout, brother Kevin said sarcastically, "Nice hit."

Next thing we knew, Larry and I were breaking up a fight.

In short, the Road to Williamsport was a lot bumpier than it had been in '92. Things nagged at me: the fracas over the trophy case, the set-to with The Parents Grim, the Pingate scandal. There seemed to be one little unfortunate happening after another.

For two years, Deborah and I had been trying to get our friends Susan and Nancy to come see an All-Star game. They finally turned up for a game in San Bernardino.

When the game was over, they left the ballpark only to discover their car had been stolen. It was found two days later in a ditch, completely stripped.

I have a feeling we may not have made Little League baseball fans out of Susan and Nancy.

Our third game was against the All-Stars of the Noon Optimist Little League, Roswell, New Mexico. They came into the tournament with a 10-0 record and having outscored opponents by a cumulative score of 116 to 17.

For all that, however, Alex held them to three hits, one of which was a single by Becky Dodson. That's right— Becky. A girl. (One of two girls in the tournament.)

We won it, 4 to 0, our runs coming on two homers by Sean. But we struggled. Their pitcher, Matt Bell, struck out 12. Crowds were larger than last year, perhaps because we were world champions, and our guys may have been a bit intimidated by the size of that night's gathering—about 10,500.

Another little unfortunate happening. And to boot, this one was entirely my fault.

Returning to the compound one night, I made two unconscionable mistakes: 1. I brought along an unopened can of beer, which was clearly against the rules, as it should be. 2. I left it on top of a locker next to a window. Anyone walking by could see it.

It was not long before Larry and I were summoned to the tournament office for a dressing-down which, in my case at least, was quite deserved. We were told it had better not happen again. It did not.

The following setbacks were physical. One of our guys, Brent Kirkland, came down with an eye infection. Brady Werner caught a virus and, with a temperature of 102, had to be taken to a doctor. A flu bug briefly hit Alex DeFazio and one of our little guys, Nate Moeiny. Luckily, all recovered quickly, but it was one more thing to worry about.

(Nate's last name unfortunately rhymes with "No Weenie," and that, of course, was the nickname accorded by his teammates.)

In our fourth tournament game, we went up against our old—and now Chick-less—rivals, San Ramon Valley. At that point, they had 16 consecutive victories. But without Chris Buchanan, their pitching star of 1992, they were not quite the same team.

Sean was being walked intentionally a lot, so we made him our lead-off man. If an opposing team wanted to walk the first batter they faced, that was their problem. San Ramon would not let us get away with that. They pitched to Sean.

He hit the third pitch out of the park.

In the fifth, they did walk him intentionally, only to have him score on a double by Timmy Lewis. The final score was 2 to 0. Sean had pitched with incredible intensity. Not until the game was over did he realize he had pitched a no-hitter.

One more victory—again over San Ramon—would send us back to Williamsport.

Our last practice at San Bernardino claimed a casualty. Al Huntley, who was helping with our coaching, likes to pitch batting practice without a protective screen. Al is Mr. Macho. Personally, I would not pitch batting practice to our kids without a screen. They hit too many screamers back at the mound.

Timmy Lewis, our left fielder, hit a vicious line drive that left Al with a choice. Get hit in the face or put his arm up to protect himself.

Al, it turned out, would be going to Williamsport with a broken arm. If, indeed, we went to Williamsport. I was beginning to think we were the Bad Luck Bears.

For our second game against San Ramon, there were 14,500 people in the stands, on top of buildings, on top of cars and trucks, and spread out on the grass beyond the outfield fence. It was the largest crowd in the 23-year history of the western regional tournament.

San Ramon got to it right away by scoring a run in the first inning. But in the second, little Jeremy Hess, a.k.a. Winnie the Pooh, tied the score with a homer.

Timmy Lewis put us ahead with a homer in the second, and the rest of the game was no contest. We won, 5 to 2.

Our guys played the best defensive game I had ever seen. Alex was the winning pitcher, but had no strikeouts.

That meant we had made 18 outs on the field. Incredible. They included great plays by the Miller twins, Brady Werner, Timmy Lewis and young Mr. Burroughs.

We recorded the final out of the tournament on a line drive that was caught by our left fielder. What made the play unique, however, was the fact that it was caught on one bounce.

It was an atrocious call by one of those umpires who probably should not even have been there. I felt bad for the other guys. Even though the other guys were San Ramon Valley.

Unaccustomed as we were to praise from San Ramon, we got it from their new manager, Gary Ryness. "Long Beach is very good," he told the sportswriters. "They have a good chance of winning it all again."

The city of Long Beach, battered by economic times and its share of racial and ethnic problems, again had something to cheer about. In the stands, one fan, Mark Betmaleck, summed it up this way:

"It brings the city closer together in a lot of ways. That's what's really neat. This team has cut across all social boundaries. Anybody that lives in Long Beach is a part of this."

Kenny and Marilou Sams had certainly made themselves part of it. Fans were still cheering when they walked out of Al Houghton Stadium and climbed into their beige Honda Accord. A teacher and teacher's assistant in the Long

Beach schools, they had thoughtfully stocked the car with changes of clothing, peanut butter and dried fruit.

They started for Williamsport, Pennsylvania. It was late Thursday night. But by driving 15 hours a day, spelling each other at the wheel in 90-minute shifts, they planned to arrive in time for Monday's 5 p.m. game against the Central U.S. team.

A year earlier, while cruising the Mississippi River, they had stopped in a sports bar in Winona, Minnesota. Having been out of touch with the news, they were startled to look up at a TV and see the Long Beach All-Stars playing in the Little League World Series.

Said Kenny, "We decided that if the team somehow went back to Williamsport the next time, we would go, too."

nineteen

BRENT KIRKLAND

Height: 5'1"
Weight: 110

A gifted athlete who played
third base and outfield, Brent
had an overall batting average
of .357 and homered during the
U.S. championship playoffs. He
got a key hit in the World
Championship game to keep
alive the team's game-winning
rally. HIt the only home run of his
Little League career in Williamsport.

We were to fly to Williamsport via a layover in Pittsburgh. This time, there would be no interminable bus ride from Harrisburg.

Watching the kids misbehave prior to take-off, one team dad, Bob Hayes, uttered something of a prayer. "I am thanking God I'm not Larry Lewis for the next 12 hours and that I do not have to watch them."

As we checked in, I had the happy experience of running into an airline clerk who was an old school chum. From TV news, he knew about the team and where we were heading. And, as a congratulatory gesture, he offered to upgrade Larry and me to first class.

Would that be fair to the kids? Would it be right for the adults to sit up there in first class, eating fine food and being doted on by flight attendants? Would it be just to leave my little guys back in the relatively cramped coach cabin?

Just about then, two of them came running past me, screaming their Little League heads off.

Yes, I decided, first class would be just dandy.

This left the kids under the watchful eye of a flight attendant, a bold swashbuckler of the air who leaped to this suicide mission as if there were medals to be earned. He even gave a little square-jawed, nothing-to-worry-about speech.

"I've been flying for years, and I've had plenty of experience in taking care of groups of kids. I've never had a problem yet. Now, you two guys just settle back and enjoy first class, and don't worry about a thing."

About an hour west of Pittsburgh, he limped back to first class with the look of a man who has just seen the Killer Tomatoes. "Those kids are out of control!" he gasped. "Absolutely out of control! Please, please, come back and talk to them. They won't listen to me."

Pretending to be astonished at this bit of news, and not wanting to tell him that they wouldn't listen to me either, I walked back to the coach section and saw exactly what he meant.

This was no longer an airplane. It was more like a tube of metal into which the contents of the world's largest pinata had been disgorged. The floor and seats were littered with a veritable hailstorm of candy wrappers, food, magazines, and more.

I gave the kids an incredibly stern lecture, knowing full well they would ignore it but figuring it might impress the adult passengers who were now beginning to realize I was connected to these urchins and were staring at me as if I were the most irresponsible grown-up on earth.

Settling back in first class again, I decided that perhaps I was.

In Long Beach, John Morris, the restaurant owner who had sparkplugged the 1992 victory parade, already was at work planning the 1993 edition.

"They haven't even won a game at Williamsport yet," someone reminded him.

"They've gone far enough," he said. "Win or lose, we're having a parade."

I was happy to be back in Williamsport and even happier to see the new facilities built since last year. Gone were the cabins. They had been replaced by modern dormitories with—unbelievable!—indoor plumbing, including showers.

"It will take a lot of effort on the part of our kids to mess this place up," I thought. Nevertheless, they gave it a pretty good try.

Four of our guys set what may be a Williamsport record. It took only two days for Timmy, Brady, Nate Moeiny, and Sean to get themselves banned from the pool.

Not only were the facilities better this year. So was the spirit. The people we met from the other teams were incredible. And with all the players now presumed to be of legal age, every team felt as if it had a chance to go all the way.

Alex Garcia, a photographer for the *Long Beach Press-Telegram*, had covered the San Bernardino tournament (and the '92 World Series). During it, he promised the players he would see them in Williamsport if they won the western title. But when they did win, another *Press-Telegram* photographer, Hillary Sloss, drew the Williamsport assignment.

Still, Garcia made good on his promise. He took vacation time and dipped into his pocket for a round-trip ticket to Williamsport.

Watching the kids had brought back memories of Garcia's own Little League days in Deerfield, Illinois. In particular, he recalled a tournament game in which he was scheduled to pitch. His parents, however, had other plans, and had taken Garcia out of town the day of the big game.

When he returned, his team, the Twins, had lost and were out of the tournament. Says Alex, "I always wondered what it would have been like...if I would have made a difference."

Just as Williamsport is the capital of Little League baseball, it is also the capital of Little League pin-trading. During World Series week, the local Elks Club serves as pin-trading headquarters.

The degree of deceit to which young pin-traders will resort was demonstrated, alas, at the expense of Jeremy Hess, who asked a local lad to watch his collection while he went to the bathroom. Needless to say, when Jeremy returned, the boy was gone and so were Jeremy's pins.

To the surprise of practically no one, the national teams for the Philippines and the Dominican Republic were caught cheating again. So was Taiwan.

Said McKittrick, our district administrator, "Those teams have cheated for years. It's hard to break old habits."

What was different this time was the fact that the teams had been disqualified. At long last, perhaps, Little League was cleaning up its act.

Ever the diplomat, Larry told a reporter, "Little League is to be commended for restoring integrity to the game. I'm sure there were some very agonizing and difficult decisions for them because it casts a huge shadow of doubt on the championships won over the last quarter-century."

There was a bit of irony. The crowning spectacular of Little League, the World Series in which we were about to play, probably would not have had the approval of Carl Stotz, the founder of Little League.

Kenneth Loss, a Williamsporter and retired newspaper editor who co-authored Stotz's biography, says, "Carl became somewhat opposed to the World Series for two reasons. He felt it...diminished the victories won at the state and regional levels. He thought state and region were as high as the competition should go.

"Second, he felt Little League had become so overly competitive that managers and even many parents had one objective—to win, no matter what the cost."

One person in the group arriving from Long Beach did not have to reset her watch to adjust to the time difference.

Sandi Lewis, Larry's wife, was wearing the watch she had purchased a year ago in Williamsport. As a gesture of good luck, she had kept it on Williamsport time the entire year.

It was, of course, a Troll Doll watch.

twenty

TRAVIS PERKINS

Height: 5'0"
Weight: 90

Probably played more positions
than anyone on the team. His
most memorable moment was the
grand slam he hit in Williamsport
in the contest for the U.S.
championship. He asks for only
three things in life: a million dollars,
a beautiful wife, and all the Little
League pins in the world.

Having groused, griped, and grumbled about the Little
League brass in Williamsport, let me now do an about-face.

Once they decided to clean up their act, they did it
well.

A month before the games in Pennsylvania, the Far
East tournament was held on the Pacific island of Saipan.
(Older Americans will remember Saipan as the island in-
vaded by U.S. forces in June 1944.)

Eight teams took part, including our old (and I do
mean old) pals from the Philippines, plus teams from Taiwan, Japan, and Korea. Also present, as I understand it,
was Joe Losch, Little League vice president and the organization's tournament director.

Prior to the tournament, teams were told they would need a host of documents—birth certificates, utility bills, photographs and more—to document the age of each player. Apparently, not everyone took this notice seriously. They had heard this sort of thing before.

This time, however, the axe fell.

As teams advanced in the tournament, they were asked for their documentation. When they could not provide it, they were tossed out. Simple as that.

Out went the Philippines. Out went Taiwan. Out went Korea.

The Far East title fell to the team from the host island, Saipan, from the Commonwealth of the North Mariana Islands Little League.

Meanwhile, the Dominican Republic was also disqualified for having overage players. Latin America would be represented by the David Doleguita Little League of Chiriqui, Panama.

For the first time in many people's memories, the playing field at Williamsport would be level.

Congratulations, Creighton Hale.

For all the criticism this book has made about Little League Baseball, Inc., let me note that the organization is to be commended for making it possible for kids to play baseball at such a high-profile level. No other youth baseball group can hold a candle to Little League.

Our first game, against the U.S. Central team from Hamilton, Ohio, was at 5 p.m. Monday. In the stands were Kenny and Marilou Sams, the couple who had driven from San Bernardino. They had made it to Williamsport with about four hours to spare before the game.

Another Long Beach couple, Gerry and Cindy Murphy, had rented a mobile home and driven it to Williamsport right after the final San Bernardino game. Apparently even more hell-bent for Williamsport than Kenny and Marilou, the Murphys stopped only to get gas.

Central was managed by Ray Nichting, a former minor league player, and coached by his son, Tim. They were a good combination, as evidenced by the fact that Hamilton had made it to Williamsport under their guidance in 1991.

We had seen the Central team that morning, and, although of legal age, they looked the size of the Green Bay Packers. Our team, on the other hand, consisted mostly of small guys, save for Timmy, Brady and Sean.

"We're playing baseball, not football," I would remind our kids. "In baseball, the fastest and most coordinated kids are the ones who usually win."

Sean pitched. From clear across the stadium, you could hear my wife, Deborah, scream, "C'mon, Burly." It was a nickname Sean had earned by virtue of his bulk.

Embarrassing as the screaming was, it may have helped. We won, 8 to 0. And Sean pitched another no-hitter.

The troll dolls were back in greater profusion than last year, and the dependence on them as good luck charms was even zanier. Taking the Long Beach people away from the smog may have affected their brains.

For one thing, all the trolls now were named "Chester," after a springer spaniel owned by Fran Sawdei, the Long Beach fan who started the "troll soul" craze.

By the final game, Sean also was being called "Chester." This only proves there are still things in baseball I do not understand.

One troll had been designated "the main Chester," and carried, in the pocket of its ragged jeans, the parents' official talisman—a token good for a free beer at the Bridge Cafe in Williamsport.

In the World Series program, there was no mention of last year's scandal. Not even a footnote or asterisk. Long Beach was simply listed as having beaten the Philippines, 6 to 0, as if a game actually had been played. (Six to 0 is the forfeit score in Little League.)

The Fiction Award of the World Series, if there had been one, would have gone to the Little League Museum next to headquarters. Its mock scoreboard from the 1992 final game showed Long Beach as having scored one run per inning.

In the barracks, it seemed as if last year's team had told the new guys that Larry and I were soft on delinquency. Telling them to shut up and go to sleep was as effective as telling a tornado to knock it off.

"Shut up, it's midnight," we would say. And one of them would answer, "No, it's nine o'clock. We're on California time."

Alex DeFazio, Charlie Hayes and the otherwise angelic Billy Gwinn lost no time in turning to a life of crime. Well, make that a few minutes of crime, during which they proved to be The Gang That Couldn't Drive Straight.

Commandeering a golf cart used by Little League functionaries, they sped off. Or attempted to speed off, only to wind up bouncing over curbs, weaving around, and driving into a building. When I spotted them and yelled, they abandoned the cart and ran off—as if I did not know who they were.

It also turned out that when they fled, the keys to the cart mysteriously fled as well. We had a pretty intense interrogation, in which I went so far as to threaten expulsion from the team if the keys did not turn up.

Alex suddenly remembered that the keys might be in the barracks. He checked. Wonder of wonders, the keys were right where he thought they might be.

Meanwhile, Timmy Lewis and Cassidy Traub were apprehended for sliding down the picturesque, sweeping hill (on cardboard) adjacent to the stadium. Caretakers were trying to keep the grass picture-perfect for national television.

Sliding down the hill is something of a local tradition, and even Williamsport grandmas have been known to indulge. Timmy and Cassidy, however, further refined the art by first sprinkling the slide path with ice.

My wife, Deborah, arrived for Tuesday's game against the South with 14 troll dolls. (She had 50 more back in the hotel room.) One, for extra good luck, was a massive troll about the size of Alex DeFazio.

It was probably a good thing she brought it along. The game was a heart-stopper.

The U.S. South team was a group of gritty, determined kids from the Tuckahoe Little League of Richmond, Virginia. Tuckahoe had a Williamsport tradition, having lost a 1-0 World Series game to Japan back in 1968.

For six innings—no, make that seven—it was Trauma City. Alex DeFazio pitched five and a half innings, and had a three-run lead when we relieved him with Brady Werner. Boom! A Richmond boy named David Henshaw tagged Brady for a homer with two on.

On the mound, Brady was thinking, "Why does this have to happen to me?" He felt he was letting the team down, and he might have felt even worse had it not been for the fact that he had hit two homers.

At the end of the sixth, the score was tied, 8 to 8.

In the seventh, which means extra innings in Little League ball, Kevin Miller led off with a homer, his second of the game. Our guys managed three more runs, and we won this very spirited ballgame by a a score of 12 to 8.

Staggering into the latrine one night about 3 a.m., I turned on the light and nearly jumped out of my skin when I saw what appeared to be a moving trash can.

As I watched, the lid of the can began to rise. And with it rose Charlie Hayes, who, upon reaching his full height, said, "You woke me up."

"Charlie, what in the world are you doing in the trash can?" I asked.

"It's comfortable," he said.

Realizing there was no future in this conversation, I turned out the light and went back to bed.

The situation by Wednesday was a bit bizarre, as often happens in double elimination competition. Only two U.S. teams were undefeated (with 2-0 records)—the U.S. East, from Bedford, New Hampshire, and your pals from Long Beach.

As the only two undefeated teams, we were assured of playing each other on Thursday for the U.S. championship. Therefore, our Wednesday game was essentially meaningless.

Which was too bad since we won the game by a score of 21 to 1.

It got to the point that I tried to hold the score down by stopping our guys, when I could, from rounding third and scoring. On wild pitches, I would hold the runner on third.

Although I do not enjoy beating any team by that kind of a score, it was still a great game because we were able to put in some of our kids who, until then, had gotten less of a chance to play than some of our regulars.

One such player was an amazing kid named Travis Perkins, who hit a grand slam and pitched the third inning.

One of the things that made Travis an amazing kid is the fact that he is a national skating champion in his age group. This is a kid who would get up at 4 a.m., skate before school, then play baseball after school. A very competitive young man.

His pitching performance in the third inning was, however, one of the strangest I ever saw. Travis, perhaps near-sighted, could not read Billy Gwinn's signals behind the plate. So rather than cross Billy up, Travis prefaced every curveball by waving his arm in a big curving motion.

Since he was pretty much throwing curves and fastballs, this meant he was telling the other team what every pitch was going to be. He retired the side on two groundouts and a strikeout. As Larry said later, "The batters probably couldn't believe that he was telling the truth."

Another strange part of the game involved Nancy Tobis. A doctor, she was late getting to Williamsport and late getting to the stadium for that particular game. She settled into her seat, and about 30 seconds later her son, Scott, hit the only home run he ever hit as a Little Leaguer.

That's the sort of thing guaranteed to bring a tear of joy to the eye of a kid's mom. Not to mention the kid's coach.

Brent Kirkland also had his only Little League home run during that game. It was amazing to think that these two kids hit the only homers of their L.L. careers at Williamsport.

I was really happy for Scott and Brent. A homer hit by a kid who almost never hits homers is, to me, one of the real thrills of Little League.

In Little League, the distance from the mound to the plate is 46 feet (reduced from 60 feet, 6 inches in the majors). At that distance, a ball at 74 mph gives the batter a reaction time of 1.2 seconds.

In the majors, a 1.2-second reaction time equates to a pitch thrown at 94 miles per hour. Someone at Williamsport clocked one of Sean's pitches at 74. Thus, he was throwing the equivalent of a major-league pitch at 94 miles per hour.

Dave Cunningham, of the *Press-Telegram*, once asked if I could get a hit off Sean. "I wouldn't face Sean," I said. "I'd beg off. It would be too embarrassing if I couldn't hit off him."

It was mind-boggling to walk through a Williamsport restaurant and hear strangers talking about our kids—using their last names, the way people talk about players in the big leagues.

"Whaddaya think? Will they pitch Burroughs in the U.S. championship game? Or will they go with Brady Werner and save Burroughs for the World Series on Saturday?"

It was an interesting question. By Wednesday night, almost 24 hours before the national title contest, I didn't know the answer myself.

For the first time since we'd been Little League-ing together, Larry and I were in major disagreement. There were no harsh words or anything like that. We just could not agree on who to put on the mound for the U.S. championship game.

To me, the U.S. title is the big game. Because of its history of fraud, the Saturday game, with the U.S. team playing a foreign team, was, to me, almost meaningless—or, at best, a sort of curiosity.

No doubt the kids did not agree with my assessment. Still, I thought that if, on Thursday, we won the U.S. title again, we could go home with our heads held high. (And with overage international players now out of the competition, the U.S. champion just might win the world title as well.) Our best chance for winning the U.S. championsip, I thought, was to have Sean pitch. He had pitched back-to-back no-hitters up until now, and his arm was still feeling strong.

But Larry wanted to save Sean for Saturday's game. He was pretty adamant about it despite my protests that if we lost Thursday, there would be no Saturday game for us. His plan was to go with Brady Werner for the U.S. title game.

Little League regulations required us to provide a preliminary line-up Thursday morning. Larry turned one · in that had Brady listed as the starting pitcher.

We continued to argue. Maybe argue is not the right word. We continued to discuss the options. I thought that if Sean did not pitch and we lost, I would never live it down. Finally, as we had done hundreds of times before, we reached an agreeable decision.

Larry explained it this way to Dave Cunningham: "The U.S. title is such a prize, we just hated to take a chance on letting that get away."

Sean would pitch.

Our fans were passionate, even if they didn't always have their facts straight. At Thursday night's game, one enthusiastic Long Beach supporter waved a sign that said: "Long Beach Can't Be Stopped."

The letters CBS were enlarged, apparently in hopes that the sign's bearer would wind up on national TV. It was a cute idea.

But the game was being telecast by ESPN.

The game that followed was nowhere close to being the paralyzing drama that the U.S. championship had been a year ago.

There was one bad moment in it, but even that wasn't real bad. In the third inning, a one-hopper bounced off Sean's glove and rolled toward second baseman Chris Miller, who could not make the throw to first in time.

The scorekeeper called it an error on Sean. And Sean agreed, saying he should have had the ball.

The call was significant. Because Sean went on to pitch his third consecutive no-hitter.

Our guys got 16 hits, including a homer by Chris Miller and two by Sean. The final score was 11 to 0.

The winners, and still the Little League champions of the United States, were the All-Stars of Long Beach, California.

twenty-one

SEAN BURROUGHS

Height: 5'4"
Weight: 125

The team's most impressive and strongest clutch hitter. Sean, son of former American League MVP Jeff Burroughs, had 16 homers in '92, including two grand slams, and batted .640 in the playoffs. With eight all-star victories, he was the team's No. 1 pitcher—and he got even better in 1993.

The most awkward part of writing this book is deciding how much attention it should give to Sean, my son.

Like any dad, I enjoy talking about my kids. But I know you have limited patience and the forests have a limited number of trees to produce these pages.

Yet, on the eve of the World Series and what would be our last Little League game together, my mind flashed back through the years of parenting.

Sean was a rambunctious guy and a rattle-thrower almost from the day he showed up; never a discipline problem, but sort of "normal wild," if that makes sense. The lad was always getting into things, always teasing his older brother (by 13 months), Scott, although they never got into a...

Well, once they did. After they had an argument one day, I told Scott, "If Sean bothers you, just retaliate." I should have realized that Scott, being only five at the time, might not have a good grasp of what was meant by "retaliate."

A short time later, I heard a horrible scream from another part of the house. Scott had hit Sean over the head with a trash can. Sean's face was covered with blood. We rushed him to the hospital and when he was cleaned up, they discovered he must have closed his eye just in time. To this day, he has a little scar on his eyelid.

Scott and I had another talk. This one was about the word "retaliate."

Shaelen, age 8, is a little Baseball Annie. She loves the game herself and is proud of her brothers. Her favorite place in the world is a ball field on which she or one of her brothers is playing.

Scott is a good ballplayer himself; he was the catcher on our 1991 All-Star team—the first team to win the district tournament in the 42-year history of Long Beach Little League. He is a 4.0 student, president of his ninth-grade class at Wilson High School, and an ace at roller hockey. "Roller Gretzky," we call him.

Deborah and I do not put Sean on a pedestal, and we make sure Scott and Shaelen see that we don't. Because of this, I like to think the self-esteem of all three is high.

Off the baseball field, Sean's activities are the usual—soccer, boogie-boarding, TV (too much of it, I'm sure), other sports, and looking up to his big brother.

I cannot pinpoint exactly when Sean showed a talent for baseball. By the time he was three, however, he was throwing and catching hard.

Marilou Sams, the Californian who drove to Williamsport with her husband, Kenny, was a teacher's aide in Sean's kindergarten class.

"We had a bean-bag board with holes in it. When it was Sean's turn, he'd back up clear across the playground and throw the bean bags right through the holes. We knew then we really had something there."

At the start of our regular 1993 season, way before All-Star tournaments, our team, the Pirates, went up against a rival club, the Dodgers. Each time Sean got up, he was intentionally walked.

It seemed this was to be the strategy of our opponents. I was ticked to think they were not going to let Sean play to his full potential, and I protested to the league. A board meeting was called over this, and I told the directors that if Sean was going to be walked each time he came up to bat, I would take him somewhere else where he could play baseball and have fun.

That was the end of that, although there were a couple of mothers who also protested that they did not want their sons batting against Sean.

In truth, Sean always watched out for the little guys, and he would lob the ball in to them. In four years of pitching, he only hit two batters. One was Alex DeFazio. In the first at-bat of his entire life.

During All-Star play in 1992 and 1993, I was always aware of Sean's performance stats. As his coach, how could I not be? He would wind up pitching three consecutive no-hitters in 1993 (one in San Bernardino and two in Williamsport). He batted .563 in the World Series. In three years of pitching Little League, he did not lose a game. In 74 innings of All-Star play in 1993, he struck out 171 and had an ERA of 0.49.

Deborah, my wife, probably does a better job of putting Sean's stats into their proper perspective. She tells him his ability is a gift from God, and that it could be taken away at any time.

She'll say, "If you wanted to paint a picture or sing a song, you couldn't do either of those things because those aren't the gifts God gave you. God gave you the ability to play baseball."

Now and then, some newspaper writer suggests that Sean is the best 12-year-old baseball player in the U.S. Personally, I would never dream of telling Sean such a thing. We usually don't know who the best is in anything. However good you are, there's always someone better.

Sean and I talk. "If you're good," I tell him, "you don't have to tell anyone you're good. You can let your ability speak for itself."

He's sensitive to what people think of him. I love those times when he'll say, "I can't do such-and-such. If I do it, people will think I'm full of myself."

For a guy his age, he is smooth in dealing with the media, even to the point of trying to enjoy himself when they ask dumb or repetitive questions. Asked by one reporter what he wanted to be when he grew up, he did not hesitate for a nanosecond.

"A gynecologist," he said.

His ability to deal with the media comes either naturally or from being around ballplayers as he was growing up. I mean, Deborah and I did not send him to the Columbia School of Broadcasting. Not yet.

I am asked now and then if Sean and I discuss his possible future in the major leagues. The answer is no. Never. However, I have told him how difficult it is to get into the big leagues and to rise once you get there.

He is 13 now. So many things can happen to him in the next six years or so. At Sean's age, sports have to be played for fun and to learn how to get along with others. The ranks of 13-year-olds should not be a training ground for professional sports.

For all that, I do remind him now and then that it would be great to help out old dad by nailing a sports scholarship to college.

My own major-league career means nothing to him. He treats me like any kid treats his dad—essentially with total disgust.

Maybe we're lucky because I have been in the big leagues. Other parents may try to live vicariously through the baseball success of their kids. But I don't have to live vicariously through my kids. I'm lucky enough to have been there.

But I think I'm better known now for being Sean Burroughs's father than he is known for being Jeff Burroughs's son.

Partway through the playoffs, Sean told Deborah, "When I have two strikes against me, I've been asking God to give me something I can hit. He hasn't let me down yet."

"Do you remember to thank him?" asked Deborah.

"Oh, yeah. I say, 'Thanks, God.'"

Okay, I never said he was glib every single minute. Besides, God is more intimidating than the media. No matter what the baseball writers might say to the contrary.

Sean came off the mound after one of his no-hitters at Williamsport and walked right into my arms. I'll carry that memory forever, but you will not find that moment recorded on the score sheets.

They haven't yet devised a scorekeeping symbol that means "one great kid hugging one dad with a lump in his throat."

twenty-two

CASSIDY TRAUB

Height: 5'0"
Weight: 90

One of those rare Little Leaguers who made his league's all-star team while only 11 years old. So determined was he to make the team that he spent much of the off-season working out in the batting cages while other kids were playing other sports. Cassidy has two ambitions: to make the major leagues and to go to heaven.

There are not many opportunities in Williamsport for parents to spend time with their Little Leaguers. Security is tight, properly so, and Little League likes to have the kids inside the compound as much as possible. Keeping them there is, in fact, one of the main jobs of the managers and coaches.

One evening, while the kids were allowed out, I went to a restaurant and ran into Jeremy Hess with his parents. After dinner, we walked back to the compound together and were surprised to find an array of police cars and a small army of police officers.

It was the very situation that League Little Baseball, Inc., dreads. One of the players was missing.

"Who?" I asked.

"Jeremy Hess."

Sheepishly, I produced Jeremy, who was standing beside me. He was in violation of the the curfew by 15 minutes, and here I was helping him violate it. We were chewed out royally for that. There were even rumblings about disqualifying us from the rest of the tournament.

Security, for whatever reason, was much tighter this year than last.

Canada's championship team was from North Vancouver, British Columbia. Along with the players came Kathy Barnard, mother of one of the team members and the first woman coach in the history of the Little League World Series. A former Little Leaguer herself, Barnard proved to be a fine coach.

The European champion this year was a repeat from 1992, the American kids from the Kaiserslautern Military Community Little League in Germany. They got to Williamsport by defeating Saudi Arabia. The whole world, it seems, is starting to play baseball.

In the international championship, Panama had defeated the American kids from Germany, 5 to 0. It was the first time in 10 years that a Latin American team had gotten into the final game.

And the first time in decades that a U.S. team was the favorite in the world championship game.

The Panamanians were ready.

"Long Beach—ugh!" a laughing Panamanian player told one of our fans the day before the game. He accompanied this brief burst of the English language by running a finger across his throat.

Actually, I had some misgivings about our being considered the favorites. I didn't want our kids to let up.

Moreover, Panama's manager, Carlos Botello Bouche, had been quoted in a newspaper as saying, "The West is a very strong hitting team. But with God, anything is possible."

Great, I thought. God's on their side.

World Series day had hardly dawned when the Long Beach contingent found that the Ticket Fiasco of 1992 had been replaced by the Ticket Fiasco of 1993. Little League had only 100 tickets for nearly 150 Long Beach fans.

Moreover, the tickets were divided; 60 in one section, 40 in another. To those of us who had become conspiracy-minded, it was almost as if someone wanted to diminish the effectiveness of our cheering section, thereby decreasing our likely number of appearances on TV.

Looking up the hill toward Little League headquarters, one Long Beach parent said, "Someone up there doesn't like us."

A Little League official assured us the organization would get the ticket problem straightened out. At next year's World Series.

We had the last practice we ever would have as a team. Before walking to the stadium for the world championship game, I called the team together for one last motivational talk.

Beyond us, I could see the stadium and the mountains in the background. Crowds were gathering on the grassy hills beyond the outfield. Thousands were milling around the stadium gates. The air was filled with electricity. Inspired by all this, I gave a talk that would have made a horse cry. It was, I thought, the perfect tone of inspiration. So touched was I by my own words that my eyes filled with tears.

"Gee, coach, get a hold of yourself," said Kevin Miller. "I mean, what a dork!"

When Brady heard he was scheduled to pitch the World Series game, he went to Larry.

"You know there's going to be something like 40,000 people here today?"

"That's right," Larry said, deliberately trying to sound calm.

"Whew!" said Brady. "And there'll be millions more watching on TV."

"Yeah, that's right."

"Wow!" said Brady. "Maybe you ought to give the ball to Alex."

But Brady took the mound.

twenty-three

SCOTT TOBIS

Height: 5'5"
Weight: 130

A player with a hot glove, Scott had his most exciting moment when he hit a home run in the United States Championship playoff—about 30 seconds after his mother took her seat in the stadium. A bright young man, he not only played well but assisted the coaching staff by picking off the opposing team's signs.

A great deal of national pride surfaces at the Little League World Series, and as we took the field a rhythmic chant began, soft at first, then louder and louder until almost everyone in the ballpark was saying it:

"USA! USA! USA!"

If a moment like that does not give you goose-bumps, tears, and a lump in your throat, you aren't alive.

Back in Long Beach, more than 400 people had jammed into Ciravello's, our pizza haunt, and they were watching the game on a legion of TV screens. The crowd ranged from teeny-boppers to Ernie Kell, the mayor of the city. "Repeat!" proclaimed a banner on one wall.

Those serving up pizza included a waitress with "L.B." tattooed on her cheeks. But our team was way beyond just being "Long Beach" now. As the first inning got underway, the crowd at Ciravello's also took up the chant.

"USA! USA! USA!"

We went through two tense, scoreless innings, the kind that may be a leading cause of heart failure in America. In the third, Panama scored and took a 1-0 lead.

We did nothing in the third, but in the fourth Sean and Brady walked. We put Scott Tobis in as a substitute runner. Our guys then advanced on a wild pitch. Things looked good. No outs. Men on second and third.

But Timmy Lewis struck out, as did Kevin Miller. Then we got some help from Panama pitcher Alex Beitia, who threw another wild pitch that scored Sean. The game was tied, 1-1.

Subdued since Panama had scored its run, the crowd at Ciravello's in Long Beach came alive again. People were standing on chairs. The chant had become, "Let's go, Beach!"

Everything seemed to be happening after two outs. We got out Panama's first two batters in the fifth, but Panama came back and got two men on. Then, on a ground ball, Sean made a bad throw from short. Panama took the lead, 2-1.

Alex Beitia had a no-hitter going into the fifth inning, when, once again, the action came after two outs. Alex singled and took second on a wild pitch. Sean walked. Brady singled, scoring Alex. The game was tied, 2-2.

If there were any place in the U.S. of A. that, at that moment, could match the tension at Howard J. Lamade Stadium, it was the home of the Tovares family, in the town of Los Alamitos, next to Long Beach.

Alejandro Tovares, 42, was pulling for the team from Panama, where he was born and raised. His son, Marcos, 10, was cheering for Long Beach. Born in the U.S., Marcos was a Little League second baseman himself.

Panama failed to score in the sixth. Timmy got a lead off single for us, then went to second on another wild pitch (Beitia's fourth). Kevin Miller bunted, as instructed, but Timmy was thrown out at third.

We put Charlie Hayes in to run for Kevin. Chris Miller singled, and Charlie went to second as the shadows lengthened in the stadium.

Up came Brent Kirkland, a nice kid who had not gotten to play all that much during the All-Star season. He had not gotten a hit in his first two at-bats, but now he singled to center. The bases were loaded.

In the course of making a substitution, Larry said to the plate umpire, "Hell of a game, isn't it? This is what Little League is all about."

Forty thousand people were on the brink of cardiac arrest, but Larry the Legend was having the time of his life. In the stands, a handful of optimistic Long Beach fans put "The Plan" into motion. They had been given packages of a pre-printed front page of the *Press-Telegram*, with a headline that screamed, "LONG BEACH WINS!"

Now, their eyes never leaving the field, they reached under their seats, broke open the packages, and began surreptitiously distributing the pages among the Long Beach fans. The idea, of course, was to hold them up for the ABC cameras should Long Beach win.

Panama changed pitchers, and their new hurler, Abel Navarro, had thrown two balls when Bouche, the team's manager, decided to change pitchers again and put his catcher, Edwin Loo, on the mound.

At this point, the collective blood pressure of 40,000 people was high enough to lift the stadium off its foundation. A lot of people had reached the point where they just wanted the game to end, no matter who won, so they could feel normal again.

But with each second now seeming like a small eternity, Loo began to take off his catcher's equipment in order to pitch.

Bouche's decision to change pitchers that quickly was, in fact, against Little League rules. The umpire told Bouche that the pitcher must finish pitching to at least one batter before a change can be made on the mound. But Bouche looked at the ump as if he were a Martian.

The problem was language. The ump spoke English. Bouche spoke Spanish. Now there was another delay as someone was brought onto the field to translate. The area around home plate looked like a Geneva peace conference.

There was still more delay as Loo put on his catcher's equipment on all over again. All those delays had to be making Panama's pitcher extra jittery, I thought. But that turned out not to be the case.

Behind on a 2-0 count, Navarro resumed pitching. From their TV booth, Jim Palmer and John Saunders agreed that there was no way we would have Billy swing at the next pitch.

I gave Billy the sign to swing if he wanted.

For months to come, I would be asked why I let him swing. Simple. I wanted him to have a chance to win the game with his bat. He's a good fastball hitter, and at that point the pitcher was going to try to throw a strike. All Billy had to do was connect with the ball, and we would have won. He deserved that chance.

Unfortunately, however, he struck out. In the stands, his mom, Judy, looked as if life would not go on.

Panama was one out away from stopping our rally and sending the game into extra innings. Nate Mociny, a good, but not strong, hitter, was due to bat. At that point, we had used 13 players. Only one man had not been played. And, although he was hitting only .167 at Williamsport, we decided to go with him now.

It was Winnie the Pooh. Jeremy Hess.

Some day, I am sure, Jeremy will learn to hit curveballs. But at this point in his life, about 6 p.m. on Aug. 28, 1993, he had as much chance of hitting a curve as he had of winning the Kentucky Derby. On the other hand, he was one of the best fastball hitters on the team.

And Abel Navarro, pitching for Panama, was throwing nothing but fastballs.

Jeremy came up to the bat looking as if he would rather be anywhere in the world than in Howard J.

Lamade Stadium with 40,000 pairs of eyes trained on him.

Larry called to him, "Nothing but fastballs, baby, okay? Get a good one."

He took a strike. Then, on the second pitch, he connected. The crowd was so tense and silent that the sound of the bat meeting the ball sounded like a rifle shot. The ball landed up against the wall in right center. Charlie Hayes scored.

Once again, we were the world champions. But this time, we had won it on the field.

twenty-four

CHARLIE HAYES

Height: 5'4"
Weight: 105

One of the team's three 11-year-olds, he scored the game-winning run against Panama for the World Championship. His exuberance upon touching the plate was captured in an award-winning photograph in the Long Beach Press-Telegram. During the regular season he hit three home runs in one game off three different pitchers.

Jeremy Hess is Mr. Unexcitement. The Duke of Deadpan. I have seen trees get more excited than Jeremy.

He came off the field after his hit looking as if he were exiting a library. One of the first people he ran into was our district administrator, Bob McKittrick.

"How does it feel to be a national hero?" asked McKittrick.

"A what?" asked Jeremy.

"You're a national hero now," McKittrick emphasized.

"I am?"

They were interrupted by a reporter, who asked Jeremy, "When you got the hit, did you realize right away what this meant?"

"No," said Jeremy. Turning to McKittrick, he added, "But he just told me."

In the stands, Jill Bratton, Jeremy's mom, was asked what she was feeling for her son. "I'm so thrilled for him, I can't describe it," she said. "What compares with this? Nothing. Well, maybe the day he was born, when I first laid eyes on him."

Victims of the bad economy, Jill and her husband, Greg, had gone through long periods of unemployment. Although they had found jobs by the time the team went to Williamsport, Jill's finances were such that she faced a dilemma. If she went to Williamsport to see Jeremy play, the expense would mean the loss of her house.

She and her family would move shortly after returning to Long Beach.

In the midst of the commotion, the ABC cameras swung briefly to the stands, showing fans holding the front page of the *Press-Telegram*. John Saunders, who was announcing the game with Jim Palmer, was impressed. "It's been printed already!"

Watching the on-field celebration from the stands, Ryan Beaver, of the 1992 All-Stars, was having mixed emotions. He was happy for the team, but he was mindful also of having been denied a similar celebration last year when it appeared the Philippines had won.

Back at Ciravello's, strangers were exchanging high-fives and hugs, chanting, "Long Beach! Long Beach!" With fans thinking ahead already to 1994, they began another chant:
"Three-peat! Three-peat!"

A third time around was not likely, however. About the instant Jeremy's line drive hit the fence, Larry Lewis made his decision.

Although he would stay involved with youth baseball at Timmy's age level, he was retiring as a Little League manager.

And, since Sean would be moving on to Pony League, it was not likely I would be back either.

It was, perhaps, the most emotional moment I'd ever known. Amid the pandemonium now unfolding on the field, the thought hit me: "It's all over. My job is done."

Never again would I be in this situation. Never again would I take a Little League field with my sons, Sean or Scott. Never again would I scale these same heights with my boys, or with all the other kids who, in a way, had also become my boys. There was nothing ahead now but memories.

A part of my life had ended.

Yet it was also a moment coaches dream about. Taking a team as far as it can go. Hugging your guys one by one on that final championship field. The odds of winning a Little League World Series are about 7,200 to 1. The odds of doing it back-to-back are astronomical.

At the press conference after the game, Bouche, the Panamanian coach, expressed confidence that, despite his team's loss, the sun would continue to rise. "All my players are sad that they are not world champs," he said. "I know all of Panama was watching. But after tomorrow, this will seem like any other game."

A writer asked why his pitchers were a bit wild while Sean was batting. Was that deliberate?

He said, "Bueno, bueno. We no want to pitch to mas grande. If we do, he hit it over scoreboard."

It was an exaggeration, but everyone laughed.

Aside from the Panamanians and their fans, there was at least one other unhappy visitor to Williamsport.

Remember The Parents Grim? Shortly after we won the final game, Mrs. Grim told a friend that the whole odyssey from Long Beach to Williamsport had been the worst experience of her life.

Her boy was a member of the world championship team. The Long Beach people were having the time of their lives. And here she was saying it was the worst thing that ever had happened to her. At times, parents astonish me.

The Little League World Series might not be the top news item around the globe. But word of it does get around. It gets around to the Pacific islands, the Far East, the Himalayas, the Middle East, Europe, and the U.S. of A.

But by that evening, it still hadn't quite gotten around to Charlie Hayes. That's right, Charlie Hayes, the kid who had scored the winning run. In the middle of our victory dinner that night, Charlie came up to me with an unbelievable question. Actually, two unbelievable questions.

"Who are we playing tomorrow, and what time is the game?"

"Charlie," I said, "we are now the champions of the world. There is no one left to play. The season is over, and we're the best."

"Oh," he said.

After dinner, we had a little celebration in a basement room of one of the motels. It was a real out-of-the-way room, and some of our people had trouble finding it. There was a little bar there, and I was standing behind it by myself when suddenly I heard a phone ringing.

Looking around, I found the phone tucked away in a little cubbyhole behind the bar. An out-of-the-way phone in an out-of-the-way place. I picked it up, and to my amazement, a voice at the other end said, "I'm trying to get Jeff Burroughs."

It was a guy phoning from Hollywood saying he wanted the rights to sell our story to television or the motion picture industry. How he found me I'll never know.

During the celebration, the adults opened a very special bottle of champagne. Given to us by one of the Little League workers, the bottle had a history. It had been confiscated last year by the L.L. after an adult smuggled it into the compound.

To celebrate the victory by the Philippines.

A final unpleasant little incident took place before we left Williamsport. One of our dear little codgers pulled the fire alarm in the compound.

This particular little codger was Sean Burroughs.

I was livid, especially since the fire marshal came out and scared us all with the threat of legal action. What Sean did was, of course, inexcusable, but not unique.

Of the eight teams there that week, we learned that ours was the fourth to sound the alarm.

At the Philadelphia airport, the kids were spotted by an elderly man from Westminster, a town near Long Beach. It was very touching. He went up to our rascals, congratulated them, then opened his wallet and gave each of them a dollar.

Checking the airport newsstands, Charlie Hayes was enthralled to discover the team on most front pages. Once on the plane, he asked every passenger reading a newspaper if he could have their sports section.

The return flight to Los Angeles was uneventful. For Larry and me. Once again, we were in first-class. (Our airline friend had taken care of us for the return trip as well.)

After two years of putting up with "The Little Team(s) That Could—and Inevitably Did," we had no compunction about retreating to the lap of luxury. Before retreating, however, we left the kids under the supervision of writer Dave Cunningham and photographer Hillary Sloss, both from the *Long Beach Press-Telegram*.

Hillary did the smart thing. She put on earphones and went to sleep—or pretended to go to sleep, not even moving when Jeremy Hess borrowed one of her cameras and began taking pictures of her.

Cunningham, on the other hand, watched the kids in stone-faced wonder as they pelted each each with peanuts, pillows, and apple chips. He watched, in fact, for a couple of hours. And then he did something he had never done in 22 years as a sportswriter.

He told a group of athletes to sit down and shut up.

Amazingly, they did exactly that. Where the heck was Cunningham for the last two years when we really needed him?

A flight attendant came by, looked at the cabin floor strewn with bits of food, and said, "I hope you guys play baseball better than you eat."

Then turning to Cunningham, the only awake adult sitting with the players, she asked, "Are you traveling with the team?"

"No," he said.

Our flight was three hours late getting into Los Angeles, but there was still an army of family, fans, autograph seekers, and media people on hand to greet us.

"This is great," said Sean. "It's party time."

While waiting for the plane to arrive, Wendy Hayes, Charlie's mother, had introduced herself to a Long Beach fan by saying, "I'm the mother of the third run."

Jim Hill, from KCBS-TV, was waiting with a limousine to take us to his station's studio for an interview. Because Jim is a fine guy and had been very good to the team over the past two years, I really wanted to accomodate him. But I had to say no.

All I wanted was to be home in my own bed. I don't think I'd ever been so tired.

Among those at the airport was fan Eva Orozco, who told a reporter how, during the 1993 season, she had prayed to her departed brother during moments when the team was struggling.

"I'd talk to him, look into the sky, whenever the boys were down. I'd say, 'C'mon, they're asking for your help.'"

Her brother was Ruben Gutierrez, the Little League umpire killed in June 1992.

twenty-five

JEREMY HESS

Height: 5'0"
Weight: 115

After a brief lesson from Al Huntley, who changed his batting stance, Jeremy belted two home runs in a game at the divisional tournament. Coming off the bench in the World Series game against Panama, with two men out and bases loaded, the kid they call "Winnie the Pooh" became a Little League immortal by driving in the winning run.

To me the most rewarding thing was not the two consecutive world championships, great as that accomplishment was. The big deal was knowing that every kid had been a part of it.

For two seasons, 1992 and 1993, we had gotten every one of our guys into every All-Star contest with the exception of one game. When you have 14 kids and only six innings per game, that is not easy to do.

Home at last, I thought of the practices, the car pools, the games and tournaments, and the Williamsport trips, in which some of our guys flew for the first time. I thought of the happy parents, the disgruntled parents, and the hundreds of hours I had spent with the kids. How fortunate I had been to be their coach. How lucky I had been to make a little difference in their lives.

Someone who has never coached may not appreciate the bond that develops between coach and player. It is the greatest experience of Little League baseball, whether your team is the world champion or last in your local league.

Let me give you a tip. If you ever get a chance to coach a Little League team—go for it. And if you don't quite know how to go about it, let me make a shameless plug here for *Jeff Burroughs' Little League Instructional Guide* (by the same publisher, Bonus Books, Inc., Chicago).

Reading it will keep you ahead of the kids. Remember: With the exception of Charlie Hayes, the kids don't read.

Once again, the Long Beach All-Stars were paraded down Pine Avenue. Marching bands. Drill teams. Showers of paper from confetti cannons.

Several thousand people jammed into the downtown amphitheater after the parade. There were a few speeches, then someone played an audio tape of Jeremy's final at-bat.

The roar the crowd gave at the sound of the bat meeting the ball was almost as loud as the one at Williamsport.

Reporters asked some of the world champions about their plans for the future. Not looking beyond the few remaining days of vacation before school, Billy Gwinn said he planned to hang around the house and watch TV.

Small wonder. Since the start of July, the kids had only had about three days off from baseball.

Jeremy's ambitions were a tad loftier. He wanted to go back to Williamsport some day and tour the Little League Museum. Although the museum is only a pop fly away from the Williamsport compound, where the players lived for an entire week, they had never gotten a chance to see it.

David Letterman's people called and invited Sean on the show Monday, September 6. Chevy Chase's people called and invited the entire team on the comedian's new (but short-lived) nighttime talk show.

The California Angels called and invited the kids to Anaheim Stadium for dinner and a ball game. There were more calls about the possibility of a movie.

There were, all in all, about 30 such invitations. We accepted some, declined others.

Sean went on Letterman's show. The host interviewed him for a few minutes, then they repaired to a New York street outside the studio. Letterman threw a few balls, and Sean belted them out to the sound of breaking glass.

Sound effects. I think.

Unhappily, the rest of the kids became victims of the TV talk-show wars. As soon as Sean appeared on Letterman's show, we got a call canceling the team's appearance on Chevy Chase's program. The producers said they just couldn't work the kids into the schedule after all. Apparently, they were miffed that Letterman had gotten one of the kids first. There's no business like show business.

A week later, the kids were on Todd Donohoe's show, which, in Los Angeles, follows "Monday Night Football." And a few months later, they drove host Ray Coombs crazy on "Family Feud."

Fame is fleeting, however. We talked to some movie people, but nothing came of it.

The following week, the kids went back to school. Larry the Legend went back to his law office. The troll dolls went back to their resting places, some in little plastic bags in which they looked like astronauts sleeping on the way to Jupiter.

Me? I went back to coaching kids. Soccer season was starting.

index

How to Play the Game

Jeff Burroughs' Little League Instructional Guide

You've just read the book about the team that beat odds of 49,000 to one to emerge as world champs two incredible years in a row. Now read *Jeff Burroughs' Little League Instructional Guide* to get specific, proven tips and techniques that will help other teams and players follow in their footsteps.

Burroughs, coach of the world champion Long Beach All-Stars and an American League MVP, offers invaluable advice on hitting, pitching and fielding, position by position. This book is the bible for Little League coaches, parents, and anyone involved in teaching and coaching young ball players. **Fully illustrated.**

ISBN 1-56625-009-9 • $12.95 paper • 157 pages

Bonus Books, Inc.
160 East Illinois Street
Chicago, Illinois 60611
(800) 225-3775